Praise for Desiree and her work in the world

Desiree has an amazing energy and spirit, especially when she talks about ancestors. She captivates with her words. I've had the pleasure of sitting with her in person, thoroughly entertained, inspired and mesmerized by her stories. I wondered why she had not written a book, and now she has, and in true Desiree style, finished it in record time. Her words are a gift at a time when we need more stories and connections to the beauty of our ancestors.

> —Monica Kenton, author of *La Novela Negra: Feminist Detective Fiction in Post-Franco Spain*. The business book I did was *Go Radical or Go Home: Be Spiritual, Make Money and Change the World*.

I had the honor of serving in Desert Storm with Desiree. Our unit was made up of Army reservists as well as active Army and our first meeting was when I was transferred in to the Kansas based unit from my Nebraska unit. Desiree made everyone feel welcomed. We were a bunch of young adults heading to a foreign country to defend and support something that was bigger than us. We were scared and stressed but Desiree seemed to take day-by-day encounters in stride. Always finding the positive. I learned that she is honest, outspoken, a great storyteller, selfless, and a very caring person. We went our separate ways after the war and unfortunately lost touch for several years at no fault to either of us, just life. Thanks to social media, we since reconnected and have become friends who participate in virtual work outs and visit frequently during the week. Not long ago, my cat had been biting me and I mentioned it to Desiree. She said that she would reach out to him to see what was going on. Several minutes later, she asked me if I had recently changed his food and if his coat was a bit dry. I replied that his coat was dry and I had changed his food a few months prior. Desiree said that Dexter felt that everything was dry and he needed his soft blanket. I was able to change his food back and found his soft blanket and within a week he was a much happier cat. Getting to know Desiree's past experiences and how she was raised sometimes leaves me in awe wondering how she stays so positive. She is who she is and I would never ask her to change. I think her purpose is to bring joy to others.

—Brenda G and Dexter!

Desiree has been the most helpful, caring, considerate and FUN medical professional I've ever had; she's always treated me like a person, not a number. I know I'll get great care from her and also that she'll make me laugh somehow. I've had these exams many times before, but this was the first time that someone did research about my condition before I even got there.

—Denise A. Romano, author of *The HR Toolkit: An Indispensable Resource for Being a Credible Activist*

Upon meeting Desiree, her genuine spirit and her sincere kindness will immediately draw you in. She is fierce in her beliefs and finds her strength in standing for them. Her love of family and friends is evident and her loyalty is strong.

If she offers you a hug, take it. Her sense of warmth and gratitude is as natural as her smile. Desiree is a true friend to many. Full of fun and laughter and always offers an easy comfort. Many, such as myself, recognize themselves as blessed to call her 'friend'.

—Carrie Scarborough Kinnard, author of *From the Grit Comes a Pearl*

Connection, Confession, Redemption
A memoir

My crazy-ass stories of
~~life, love, and legacy~~
~~wine, women, and woo-woo~~
~~military, family, and career~~
Self-Acceptance

Desiree B.

ISBN: 978-1-7358881-0-1

Copyright © 2020 by Desiree B.

Printed in the United States of America. All rights reserved under International Copyright Law. Contents and/or cover may not be reproduced in whole or in part in any form without the express written consent of the Publisher.

We are all born into something.

What we do with what we learn, who we learn it from, and who we teach is up to us.

JOURNAL ENTRY

March 1998

> *It's all I can do to breathe in this day.*
> *I'm hooked on this living thing*
> *and I want to consume it all*
> *by wasting nothing, and frightening my life.*
>
> *I wish you could spy in at everything I've seen and done.*
> *Not everything I love is "good."*
> *Some of the wickedness supports me like oxygen.*

1

When I was a kid, I was the youngest of five. I grew up on a hobby farm. Meaning, we didn't have income from the land or the animals. The farm was a side project for my stepdad, who made regular decent income as a pipe fitter. We did not know that the income was fine though. We lived our lives as if we were a family dependent on what we could produce. I don't recommend it. It does not give a sense of security.

Security. That's kind of been a thing for me.

There was love in our family, but there was also a lot of jockeying for position, like in the game "Survivor." I used to hide out a lot. Figuratively and literally. In the summertime my favorite spot was in a hollowed-out old tree. In the winter, I hid in an underground snow tunnel or in any area that I carved out myself in a big snowdrift. Oh yeah, I grew up in Minnesota. We had plenty of snow.

Mom said I was scared of people and that when the mailman came, or the milkman, or whoever, I held onto the back of her legs and cried. She also said I was always pretty quiet and that I couldn't say shit if I had a mouthful of it. I didn't speak up for myself much. Or speak out against any wrongdoings against others. Man, I've sure made up for my childhood!

I was a young twenty-something, working at a cheese packing plant when I finally did in fact have shit to say.

As far as the plant went, it was a good time. We made Muenster cheese for Little Caesars. There was a gift shop out front that sold some cheese, and a lot of local meats and other local stuff. I worked the 2:30 a.m. to whatever p.m. shift, in the packing and shipping area. We pulled 11-pound wheels of cheese out of brine vats and put them on a conveyer belt where they'd run along from there until they went through a metal detector. Dropping into a plastic pocket, the cheese wheels were sealed, weighed, and then boxed up by the last person. The pallet of boxes were forklifted outside, to a stand-alone cooler.

We were a bunch of 20-year-olds who were out to have a good time. Every Friday, the guy in the lab that tested the cheese announced over the speaker system that there was pizza to eat. If we had 11, 12, or 13 different vats of cheese then that's how many pizzas we had. One wheel of cheese was tested from each vat. Sometimes the supervisor was super nice and took some pepperoni from the gift shop and put it on a pizza. I also got free Pepsi. Whenever someone got a Pepsi from the vending machine there was always another can that got hung up. If you don't know about old-school pop machines or don't remember, there was a can shoot. You could reach your hand up there a little if you wanted to catch your soda coming down. Fairly often, a can got stuck at the start. My arm was small enough that I could reach up in there to grab that lodged can. Free Pepsi, free pizza, life was okay.

We had a good time messing with each other, and with the metal detectors and the big hoses that cleaned up the shop. Imagine walking along and suddenly getting hit with a huge deluge of water, trapped in a doorway, getting hit from all sides by three different water hoses. Or picture someone stacking up boxes of cheese on a pallet, and someone else runs by and gives a good push so that guy or girl is right up against the boxes. Someone else immediately is there with the big rolls of pallet wrap and literally wraps them to the boxes. Teamwork at its finest! One day we decided to have fun in the gift shop area and we wrapped one of the secretaries to her chair (and all of her folders of work with her when she said, laughing, that she had a lot of work to do). It was also not uncommon to go to the parking lot at the end of a tiring shift, only to see your car completely wrapped up tight.

At the station that weighed the cheese, we all took delight in taking the large cutting knife (used to trim larger wheels of cheese so they'd fit into the plastic pockets) and passing it underneath the metal detector so that the conveyor belt stopped. That created a huge logjam of cheese wheels flying all over the floor. If you can picture Lucy and Ethel stuffing candy everywhere, think 10-pound wheels of cheese!

One time I came around the corner and the guys had a friend of ours upside down over the whey tank. We knew that change had fallen out of his pocket. And ended up in the cheese. So we only had to wait until the cheese with the money came to the conveyor belt and hit the metal detector. We laughed so damn hard. I only hoped it didn't come through when I was manning the cheese sealer/metal detector.

Stupid shit like that never got old.

Another funny thing at the plant (so many!) was the brine vats. We'd lean over them, and even with our aprons, our shirts got wet, leaving big circles of salt around our boobs. Too bad selfies weren't a thing in those days. We also took our salty gloves and wiped them on the lenses of anyone who wore glasses. It was tough as shit to get salty brine water off of your glasses while working, not being able to see. It made it tough when leaving the shipping area with a forklift full of cheese boxes. We'd also pull pranks and hit the "door down" button just when someone was coming in or leaving through that garage door. Forklift marks peppered the door. We also used the forklift in the parking lot to whip each other around, spinning in circles when it was icy out there.

Then there's the time when my then-girlfriend gave me a hickey on my forehead. She knew I had to wear a safety hairnet and with my big high forehead everyone at work was able to see my hickey for days.

Even though I had a girlfriend, there was a woman at work (or rather girl, I should say, since we were both stupidly young) who caught my eye. I tried to hang out with Kim during and after work as much as possible. We got drunk most days after quitting time. Now mind you, we were in the Kansas Bible belt. People didn't view kindly to gay people. This was 1989, so for sure it was difficult. In that same timeframe, there was a girl up in Nebraska that was beaten and murdered for being gay. We heard about it via the underground newspapers. Later on, the movie *Boys Don't Cry* was based on this event. Assault by cowards.

Cowards who were afraid of what they did not know anything about, felt their norm threatened.

At any rate, Kim was making me mad at work and I finally found my voice. It was actually at the end of a water and cheese fight. A piece of equipment was not working, so we attempted to fix the PVC pipes ourselves. We were all hurling soft items, as one does in a cheese chunk fight, when I felt something hard hit my forehead. I looked up with my eyes, seeing something there as it unstuck from my forehead, falling to the floor. Suddenly, blood rushed into my eyes and all down my face. That wasn't a piece of cheese that hit me.

We had to figure out a way to tell the supervisor how I "accidentally" got a piece of broken PVC stuck in my forehead. There was no way of hiding it, since we wore those damn hairnets. I laughed at the incident, but also was pissed because Kim should have known better, and really could have messed me up. So we got pissy at each other. I stood up for myself. Standing up for myself was a new thing and felt strangely wonderful.

Kim and I ended up having an affair. I wanted to leave the woman I was seeing, so I could date Kim exclusively. I didn't get that chance. On New Year's morning 1990, Kim called me to say goodbye.

"I love you. I'm going to kill myself. I have your Army dog tags around my neck. I will always love you. I'm sorry. Goodbye."

I could hear my beloved Concrete Blonde music blaring from a distance on her prize-winning stereo in her car. Then she hung up.

Kim actually went through with it.

My ex got a phone call a little later from the police asking for me. I got on the phone and they asked me what I looked like. I was confused. They told me somebody not matching my description had my dog tags around their neck and was dead. They asked me to drive to the police station there, a neighboring city, to give a statement.

I was in shock for days. I was so pissed at the police there. They had received a phone call about a gunshot from near Kim's residence, but said they found no reason to investigate. They supposedly cruised by but said they did not see anything suspicious. The car stereo outside was blasting so loud, I could hear it on the phone inside when Kim called. Wouldn't that have been something to check out? An empty car with loud music? The screen door was torn (from a previous break in, but would the cops know that?). A neighbor heard a gunshot. Yet the police found nothing out of the ordinary for 0520 in the morning? I don't think they even drove by.

There actually had been two gunshots. According to the police report, when Kim shot herself, she did not have the angle right, with her petite arms and long shotgun. She crawled across the floor to pick up the shot gun to shoot again and finish it.

I've had dreams with Kim in them. In one, we were meeting up at an outdoor patio restaurant. Kim was with two sunglasses guys. They seemed to be her guards or something of that sort. When we sat down, I said right away that she was dead, and asked what was going on. She replied that yeah, she was dead, but wanted to check in with me. Like it was normal for a dead person to go on visits.

I know that dreams are powerful, and I have learned a bit to control the dream, when I realize it's a dream. I try to get information, or ask questions. Learn from it. Kim and I chatted, but I don't remember exactly what all was said. Only that she was dead, and was checking in.

I will never forget all that I learned from her. How to speak up for myself. How to go for what I want. What suicide does to loved ones. That what we think others think of us is often wrong and also none of our business. Kim felt no one cared for her, that no one loved her. Her funeral was three hours away, in a snowstorm so bad that we thought it would shut highways down, and yet the church had standing room only. Standing. Room. Only. So many people. And she thought no one loved her. It's messed up.

I'd think of her stupid suicide several years later, when a co-worker killed himself. And again, in 1998 when I myself sat there with a shotgun.

2

Yes, I will tell you about my own suicidal thoughts, but obviously I'm still here so it's not much of a cliffhanger, is it? Let me stay with this train of thought, for now. Later that same year in November, I was activated for Desert Storm. I was in the Army Reserves, and my unit was notified at our regular monthly drill weekend that were being called to active duty. The day before, us kids at the cheese plant were told the plant was closing. How's that for a kick in the ass?

Anyone wanting to stay on with the cheese company had to move to Joplin, Missouri. That didn't sound too exciting. I was relieved that I had job lined up with the military, but man, it was scary to think about going "over there" to the desert.

Before going overseas, I first had to report to Fort Riley, Kansas. The fulltime military people gave us Reservists a lot of shit. I've heard so many times over the years that we don't matter, that we aren't doing a "real job," that we are "just Reservists." Being pulled out of our civilian jobs, civilian way of life, changing up our every waking moment is not easy. At least fulltime military put on the same uniform, answer to the same chain of command, work in the same job field. They know about temporary housing, living arrangements, etc. Some of them, I think, sign up fully aware that they might go to war, and are more prepared for it. That was never my plan. The only thing about going to war that I found was an actual good thing, was that I was going with some of my best friends. I had friends that I'd made in our Reserve monthly weekends (and two weeks a year trainings) that I hung out with a lot outside of those Army times. At least we'd be in this together.

It was so damn cold on that Fort Riley base, as the barracks were from WWII and had not been updated much. Drafty. Crappy plumbing. Rock hard beds. Since a lot of us knew each other, it was nice to hang out with familiar faces. My friend Monica read the book *Misery* to a couple of us at night while we snuggled under a shitty wool military blanket. We played cards a lot, and smoked a lot. We were supposed to smoke outside, since the old decrepit building could catch fire in a split second. Instead, we smoked on the little balcony area at the top of the stairs. We had daily morning and nightly formation (you know what formation is—lined up for roll call, like you see in movies). Every morning, the First Sergeant announced "…Building 2487, PLEASE STOP SMOKING." Telling young 20-something punks this every single day. What a joke. I thought it was funny. But I admit I learned a lot there.

For the Reserves, I was an x-ray tech, but obviously I didn't like working in the x-ray field since I chose to work in the cheese plant rather than at an x-ray job in my civilian life. Still, I was promoted to sergeant right before we went over. Our hospital needed someone to be in charge of our radiology department. There was a staff sergeant already, but he really didn't know what was going on. So, the powers-that-be decided to let a 22-year-old who didn't even work in the field be in charge, during a war. Brilliant. A nurse in our unit did radiology as a civilian so I asked if he would help me get our department up to speed. I needed to know how to set up and run the equipment, how to manage the staff that I would have. He was willing to help me out, and he was wonderful.

One piece of equipment we were getting was the first of its kind. A field unit fluoroscopy machine. This is the machine that's used to image a person while doing something, like swallowing barium. I was sent to San Antonio to get special training on how to put one together, once in Theater. Theater meaning once over there, in our physical location during the war. The machine was to be stored in a wooden box, broken down to fit. The box would go into an ISO, a large storage container, a shipping container size. Each department had these ISO containers. Radiology had three, but someone higher up in command took one of ours to use as an administration office, so we only had two. But, in Theater, I made it work. I put one on each end of the hospital. One was near surgery and the emergency room. The other was put near the nursing halls, so we could do portable exams and develop films easier. It was also strategically near the dinner area.

I scheduled our department to work 24 on and 24 off. During my 24 on, I got pretty good at doing portable x-rays on people that had body parts blown up by shrapnel. Including women and children. Time is of the essence when dealing with so much trauma. We truly had one shot to get some images for the doctors before the patient was either transferred out to Germany, or sent to our surgery. On duty that Easter, we had a case where a kid took a bullet to the head. It was a lucky lucky break though because the bullet was lodged in his sinuses. The neurosurgeon that worked on him was a world renowned surgeon. I don't know if this doc was activated for Desert Storm, or volunteered, but we were lucky enough to get him. He let me step up on to a riser so I could get a good look at the bullet and watch him work. Very cool.

There are endless stories from my time there, but let's keep this light. One reason I scheduled 24 hour shifts was so I could sleep in the A/C. This was the desert, after all. I had a blowup pool floaty that I put on top of one of the x-ray tables, and I slept there. I also told Supply that I needed a refrigerator to keep my IV contrast cold. That's a damn lie. X-ray IV contrast needs to be in a warmer, so it's less viscous, but they didn't know that. I had air conditioning and a refrigerator—in a WAR. Me and my bestie walked around the hospital with our neon green cups that we'd brought with us from home and people almost got whiplash hearing the sound of ice cubes in our cups.

You gotta make fun times when it's a shit show.

I also got a good tan, as I had brought my bikini. Yeah, that wasn't on the list of things to pack. After the official war was done, my buddies and I laid out in the sun. We got someone to announce overhead every thirty minutes "sunbathers it's time to turn over." I decided I would only go outside on my days off when the tent thermometer (why in the hell did we have a thermometer in the desert??) went above 100 degrees. I figured I might as well get a tan if I had to be hot as shit. It was so hot that when I hung out my uniform to dry, it only took ten minutes. These were winter uniforms, mind you, especially thick in the pocket folds. And they dried that fast. We were issued only one pair of desert uniforms. One. And no desert boots until the actual DAY before we left. We were told that we WOULD wear those boots for any photo ops when we landed back in America. Whatever. (I still have those boots. I like to wear them for projects outside, as I live in an area that is HOT all the time.)

In the military, you'll do well if you get along with Supply. You get extra stuff if you ask nicely. Also high on the list to be chums with are the Human Resources folks (why is my pay messed up, or, how can I get promoted?), and of course, anyone and everyone in the Mess Hall. Getting slices of baloney, canned goods, and extra desserts ruled the day.

People in Supply and the Mess Hall did various errand runs off of our compound with a two-and-a-half-ton ("deuce and a half") truck. We had a "gay day" run once. Word spread through camp that if you were gay, meet up at the Mess Hall at 0800. We took off secretly into town. We had some damn good chicken and rice, bought some souvenirs from the street vendors from Kuwait, and laughed when we knew our gaydar was correct by seeing who was along for the day.

In addition to the Reserve friends I already knew when going over, I also made good friends while there, since I had to go into all areas of the hospital for portable exams. You get close in ways you could never think of when you're in war together.

We had outdoor showers, in these curtained off areas, over pallets. During a sandstorm, we traveled as buddies, lined up, one hand on the shoulder of the friend in front of you, eyes closed to keep the sand out, but hanging on tight. Otherwise, we would not even know where to go. Speaking of "going"—women, as you might already know—we often like to go to the ladies room together. Being over there was no exception. We'd go together, and hang out in the 2 and 3 seat area. Now, these latrines were see-through from chest up, covered by screen. So you could see anyone from afar. And I guess they could see you. We didn't care. It was good that it was so open, because besides the ever-present cigarette, it smelled like shit in there.

A lot of us got dysentery, from whatever. So. One time I was there in the outhouse, alone, doing my daily duty. Up comes a truck and a trailer, it was the porta staff. Their job was to open up the back of the latrine, exposing the 3' high/3' round steel containers that they had to dump and burn. The stalls had plywood up the back, so they could not see if anyone was in there. I did not say a damn thing. I sat there quietly and did my business. With dysentery, it was impossible to hold it anyway. I heard a "GOD DAMMIT!! WHO THE FUCK IS IN THERE? YOU DROPPED SHIT THAT WE GOTTA PICK UP!"

I laughed so hard. I knew that voice. To this day, I'll bet he knows it was me, but will now know for certain, if he reads this. Oh my, that was funny. I felt bad, but jeesh!! Speaking of having the shits, at the end of the war, the threat of getting gassed had passed so in our hip-strapped gas mask bag, a lot of us (not just women) put two rolls of toilet paper in there in place of our masks. You had to be ready all of the time for that run to the porta potty!

Desiree B.

Our average age was 25 so we liked to make things fun when we could. People went swimming in the water bladders, lots of late night laughter, and there were plenty of practical jokes. In formation one morning, I looked over at a deuce and a half truck parked nearby. On the side, glaring at us in the early morning light, in black spray paint was written: "What the fuck? Over!"

I knew for a fact that the Hoe Dogs had gotten in trouble for saying that over the telephone communication systems and I knew this prank had to have been done by a HD (Hoe Dog, what most of the women in our tent named each other). I was so proud of her, whichever HD it was, who painted that truck.

I kept a small spray bottle near my cot that I used most mornings to spritz water on my hair, to help smooth it out before heading into work. One morning, I sprayed as usual. I smelled cherry, and saw red streaks coming down my face. I was at once pissed (sugar all over, and now delayed by having to fix WTF was going on) and proud of the HD that did this. Monica, the excellent jokester! The laughter with her across from me during the war was so needed. I'm thankful for all of the everyday bullshit. I have a series of photos of the HDs that worked on the nursing floors. Each one is flipping me off. Very professional, ladies. And I love you.

Of course we had drinks, even though it was illegal to drink in Saudi. I was on guard duty one night, and some drunk Brits came through. I got to talking to them, and said I had a buddy who was turning 21 the next Wednesday. If they could come back, bring some alcohol. They came back Monday, and Tuesday, and the rest of the week. Man, we partied! They made an Ouzo cake. Not good, but the attempt was appreciated. We made wine in the X-ray dark room, too. There were large jugs of water for the film processors. I'd gotten a wine starter from one of the officers. The wine being made needed to be in a clean, dark environment. The dark room was perfect. The wine did not turn out very tasty but it had a little punch. At the end of the war, we Hoe Dogs sat around and enjoyed that crappy homemade wine and toasted to it all.

We made meals together, being imaginative with MREs—"Meals Ready to Eat." Some of the main courses were not too bad. I think the BBQ-something was my favorite. I liked getting the crackers as a side, with peanut butter. One of the standards that most soldiers know is the "Ranger cookie." Carefully open two sugar and creamer packets. Mix half and half the best you can in the creamer packet (the creamer packet had a foil wrapper under its paper wrapper). Fold down tightly. Using the matches that came with the MRE, set fire to the bulky sugar/creamer foiled pack. When the paper burns away, the heat melds the two ingredients. Peel away the foil, and voila! A sugar cookie!

There was a fairly local PX, or Post Exchange. We did not get to go often, so we'd stock up when we could. Or send money with others if they were going. Microwave single servings had recently come onto the market. Those were popular, as they stored well, and with the pull off top, were easy to eat. I had a case of Mountain Dew under my cot. I don't remember how I got a whole case of it, but it was like gold! Also crazy and fun were the paper/foil cans of snacks. Doritos, cheese balls, etc. were in a container like Pringles, but it was short and fat. I reused the containers to keep some of my stuff sand-free. Even in the tent, fine sand was everywhere. I used the wooden crates that some of the x-ray equipment came in, for my own shelving/dresser. You could also use a cardboard box, some string and/or duct tape. Turn the box on its side, and put cardboard shelves in. Nice place to store clothes, etc. Also popular were the large popcorn tins we'd receive from home. Easy to wipe out and reuse to keep sand out.

On the side of my crate "nightstand," I had a battery-charged alarm clock that I'd had since Basic Training, eyeglasses, and the bottom half of a water bottle filled with sand. It was my ashtray, easy to dump and refill every day. Quite convenient when in the desert. Water bottles were a fairly new concept for us Americans back then, because why would someone buy a bottle of water? But there, much appreciated. We were lucky, as once a week, a refrigerated semitruck arrived. We waited in line for up to an hour, in the heat, to exchange hot water bottles for equal number of cold ones. Silly really, since by the time we got back to our tent, they'd be hot again.

We Hoe Dogs set up a nice area in our tent. I used one of the longer crates as a "living room" table for us. We arranged cots, cushions, and a short large bucket type thing that we used both for storing stuff under our cots, and for filling with water to clean up/shave. We sat around chatting, all of us shaving our legs.

We also had ropes, spread across the aisles. We hung stuff there to dry. We made sure that whenever the First Sergeant came through for whatever, we had ALL of our bras and underwear hanging from those ropes. HAHAH! It was so funny, seeing him walk through, carefully moving the pieces of undergarments, like moving through a jungle full of hanging snakes. When a few of the HDs came to my home twenty years post-Desert Storm, I made a makeshift rope across the entrance near my front door. I hung up my undies, bras, a bikini. Set nearby was the one set of desert camouflage uniforms that I'd had, and of course the desert boots received the day we left. I also hung the part of the tent that I'd taken with me. We all used magic markers and drew on the ceiling above our cots. Great for decoration, but also good for identifying whose was whose cot. The HDs loved my welcome for them!

When I got back to the US after my deployment, I went on unemployment for three months. I loved being free for a while, staying connected with the friends that I was used to seeing 24/7. Then I applied for an x-ray job when one opened up at a local hospital. I had no idea how that would change my life, for the better.

I found that I like the brain work that is medical imaging. I also love taking care of people. I love to calm people down after they've been in an accident, or when they just got the news that they have cancer, or when they are just plain scared to have any kind of imaging done. I've been doing imaging now for over three decades. I absolutely love it. I get to stick people with an IV, and then stick them into a tube. My goal is to do it without them being too afraid.

Back then I could not imagine how life would turn out. But I like it. It kind of brings me to the writing of this book. Never thought this would be a project I'd take on. I told my editor that I'd much rather have a wiggling four-year-old to start an IV on because I can do that way better than writing a book. But here I am, writing my stories, and it's good to get it out.

3

I'm not sure how this began for me, but I've always felt the need to help people. And sometimes I can get too close. I think it's called being codependent.

I'd been dating a woman for two years and proposed to her over Valentine's weekend. Yeah, corny. It was a Civil Ceremony, not legal, but the closest we could get to a "real marriage" in Kansas. Marriage wasn't legal yet in 1997.

Sue and I had a great time together, laughing, traveling around the Midwest, and down to Mississippi to see her family. I decided that yes, I loved her, and this was the best relationship I'd had so far, so why not get married? Was I in love with Sue? No. But it's not something that I let myself think about.

The marriage was a mistake. I knew that for sure a few months later, even before we got married. During our one-year engagement, actually only a few months after I'd proposed, I met a woman, Jenny, who I instantly fell in love with. Jenny and I had quite the impact on each other's lives. Twenty years later she and I would talk about this, try to make some sense of it all before she died.

About 6 months later, Sue and I went to see Jenny, who was a mutual friend, not just mine, who had moved to France. I was a stupid 29-year-old who should've known better. Jenny and I had been writing to each other and sending emails, getting to know each other more. In so many ways. I was drawn to her, as I know a lot of people were. It was interesting, how many people around her felt her presence, wanted more of it. What was different for me was that Jenny responded back. Jenny made me feel special, and that she and I had something special.

While there in France, I also visited Germany and traveled by train through Switzerland. I found my love for train travel, and eating chocolates in different countries. I loved going to markets and grocery stores to see what the local people ate and did, including what kind of toothpaste they used. I found that I enjoyed speaking to local people in their language, using the best "hello, thank you, and one more beer please!" that I could muster, wherever I was.

Traveling by train was brilliant. Feeling excitement the whole time, it was like traveling in a car, but so much faster, my speed of seeing things. I imagined the French cows, knowing French commands. Seeing a Swiss cat, knowing the cat understood a language that I did not. I journaled a lot and preferred to sit in a car by myself if possible. Writing, drinking a coffee, a tea. Having a Gauloise, the brand that Jenny smoked, and that I had too now for many months. A porter came through the train car now and again, with a cart full of chocolates, sweets, etc. I knew when the train was in a different country, by the offerings. Euros were not used yet, so I had a good time pulling out my coins and notes from different countries to pay for my stuff. During one leg of the trip, I sat next to a guy from Dijon, France. I had no idea until then that Dijon was a place, not just a mustard. LOL. I spoke shitty French, he knew no English. We enjoyed each other's company anyway, pointing out things we saw while on that route. I had the time of my life traveling around Europe. But when I got back to Paris, the shit hit the fan.

Jenny and I stayed out late. Or maybe it was early, as we'd closed the town down. The Metro was not even running at that hour, so we walked, enjoying all the love around that is Paris. Sitting on the steps of the hotel, smoking our Gauloise cigarettes, we talked and laughed.

Everyone smoked there, all over. Including the Frenchman who rode up the elevator with us. Me with my too-big American-sized bag, Jenny, this 6-foot Swedish blonde that looked like a large German, and the chain-smoking little man, we looked like a scene from a comedy skit. As we got into the tiny lift, there was barely enough room for two people, let alone all three and my bag. The Frenchman ignored us, smoking, seemingly many cigarettes in such a short time. I looked up at Jenny, and imitating his face, I lit a cigarette. We thought it was all so damn funny—the cramped spaces, the man needing a shower, her towering above both of us, my American-ness, and the European penchant for smoking every damn where—and we tried to not laugh, but it was impossible. The lift doors opened on the next floor, and looking like a Cheech and Chong movie as we stepped out, billowing smoke, we fell out onto the floor in a heap of laughter.

About a week later, Jenny and I sat on the carpeted stairs of this beautiful old Paris hotel, talking carefully about our relationship, how it had progressed over our six months of letter writing, and the time before that at her apartment before she'd left for France, and now that we were here together. I told Jenny that I loved my wife, but was not in love with her. I had married Sue for the wrong reasons. I'd felt it was "the next step" that I was supposed to do. But when I met Jenny, I knew what being in love was really like. That I'd felt my world turn upside down, because I did not know what to do with love at first sight. But I did not know how to uncouple my current relationship. We had in-laws, friends, a home. I didn't know how to not hurt Sue. I also knew there were things I had not liked about her, things I thought I could "fix" somehow. Of course there were things Sue did not like about me, so why had she agreed to stay with me, too? It all came to a head while in Europe together. I felt trapped, and we all felt it, felt that the marriage was wrong. I wanted to stay in Paris with Jenny, and I should have. I should have not stayed with Sue for so damn long. It was obvious that we both deserved someone else, someone better.

Back then, I felt I always needed to be in a relationship. Being single was difficult. And I did not really know how Jenny felt before she had left for school in France. She did not verbalize it, only hinted at it with beautiful letters, poetry, French tea, and photos that she'd send. This long night in Paris, I was angry because I needed to know, verbally, what she felt. I yelled at her to tell me what I truly meant to her. Jenny yelled at me, feeling hurt that I did not do the right thing, did not do right by her.

Sue heard us, as she was up the stairs in our room. She'd been there for a couple of days, not wanting to go out and travel around with me or even explore Paris. Her desire to stay back had nothing to do with me and Jenny, but was the usual "I don't want to do it, so I don't have to, I can ruin it for everyone if I want to." An attitude that I was so sick of for the whole relationship, made wholly apparent now.

Sue asked me what we were arguing about.

"We're trying to figure out what the fuck is going on."

"Is Jenny in love with you?"

I said yes.

"Well," Sue replied. "That's too bad. Quite the fucked up situation, isn't it?"

She never asked me if I was in love with Jenny. I know now she did not have to.

When we got back home, our civil marriage split up, and not just because of Jenny, but for reasons that should have split us years earlier. Sue and I still chatted most nights and drank wine together, feeling sad that we'd not be around each other anymore laughing, but not sad about the marriage, about being a couple. Odd, for sure, but we knew we never should have stayed together.

I awaited the return of Jenny. I had fallen for her completely. And I mean completely. My only focus was this relationship. Jenny was always on my mind. ALWAYS. Our relationship ended up being one of the most spectacular, but also detrimental, relationships of my life.

That night in Paris, Jenny never told me, exactly, while sitting on those stairs, that she loved me. She never said the words, but her eyes and actions, and all those letters and emails, had told me. I loved Jenny. Jenny loved me. We continued our long distance relationship and grew even closer. Or so I thought. Jenny's schooling ended and on her way back home to the states, she met a guy in the airport. I told you she had a way of having people drawn to her. The dude was head over heels for Jenny. I never knew exactly how Jenny felt about him, but she kept him around. Brian seemed to be her pawn, and in a way I felt sorry for him. He was nice, fun, and yes, I'd met him a few times. Jenny went back and forth with dating both of us. And both Brian and I put up with it.

Jenny felt torn, she told me, trying to tell me one day that she loved me, and the next, no phone calls, no communication. I was a yo-yo on her string. But I stayed. I stayed focused on Jenny. It wasn't enough.

Life was hard enough, but being in love with Jenny was kind of like my drug. Jenny would be with me one whole weekend; the next she would fly to Atlanta to be with Brian. The back and forth and yes and no that I got from her messed with me very badly. It's not easy to fully describe how I much I lost myself, but I started talking out loud to myself, and I couldn't eat, I couldn't sleep. I lost a lot of weight. It became quite difficult to lead a normal daily life. I journaled a lot which helped. I also started seeing a therapist. I think therapy is important. I also think that more people should do therapy just for the heck of it. My therapist and I talked a lot, about codependency, family life, other relationships. There was a sense of abandonment I felt that came out. It's plausible, and I will fill you in on that origin, but it also felt weird openly talking about it. But I know that working with my therapist helped me. It helped me to realize that there was something inside of me that made me feel this way, letting me know that I could change it. But it was difficult finding how to change it.

There were some other difficult things happening at the same time. Beside Jenny being with Brian, Jenny's mother said she would cut off her college and travels if she dated "that woman." Me. So for a bit, Jenny said she needed to break it off with me. I'd been hanging out with a mutual friend, David, who in my opinion, was also in love with Jenny. Yeah, she was that magnetic. I stayed at David's place one night, after drinking too much to drive home. His alarm clock went off in the morning. The alarm was a song from my beloved Concrete Blonde called "Jenny I Read." I laughed, knowing he'd been waking up each day with thoughts of both me and Jenny. David had slept on the floor, on a mat he'd gotten in India. Laughing at the song, I rolled off the bed, onto him. I ended up sleeping with David.

We had a short relationship, actually a lot of fun. He was smart, funny, and loved to travel, too. We talked about the possibility that I could get pregnant. We agreed to stay together if I did. I knew that even though I felt all of these wonderful things with him, it could never be the same as the filling relationship that I had with women because life has responsibilities for our actions. I was a lesbian who did not like to be alone. And I was still immersed in my world with Jenny.

Let me interject a funny side note. Months before I slept with David, we'd traveled to Pittsburgh together, with a couple of his friends. We wanted some alone time in the hotel room. We were pals and enjoyed the shit out of each other. We decided the bathroom was the perfect spot to go. We jumped in the bathtub and hung out there. We ran a hot bubble bath and just relaxed. We sat in the tub, lights low, talking, laughing. We didn't care what his

Connection, Confession, Redemption

friends thought. I was comfortable with him, and he I, and whatever, we did not care. We were two besties doing what we wanted. We had no idea how long we'd been sitting in the tub, chatting away, but eventually we both realized at the same time that all of the water had drained out! We laughed our asses off.

When we came out of the bathroom, laughing, the others asked what the hell we'd been up to. We said we took a bath and chatted. They did not believe us. The young, smart man, and the eight years older lesbian. Yeah, right, they said.

Truth is stranger than fiction sometimes.

But later on, we did have sex. We liked each other immensely and both were lonely. Hell, straight people have friends with benefits. Why can't I? But the end part of our relationship was sad. Turns out I ended up having a miscarriage. To make it worse, the OB/GYN nurse told me that it was "a good thing" because I was a lesbian and probably wouldn't keep the baby anyway. How can someone be so cruel! I was going crazy over my (I guess) codependency issues, freaking out over my love for Jenny, and losing a pregnancy and told this inhumane bullshit.

I was at my breaking point.

I had to either get my life together ... or do something drastic.

4

During this time of anguish over Jenny, the miscarriage, being treated like shit for being gay, life in general being shitty, I was also studying for the Magnetic Resonance Imaging (MRI) national registry. It was the first time it was being offered. I did not go to school for MRI, just learned on the job. I'd also ordered the 1st edition of an MRI physics book to learn from. A lot of the book was theory for me though, because our scanner was not that advanced. There were things that I knew we could do, but not how to do them yet. My brain was struggling to make sense of my relationships, and how to literally not go more crazy, and also studying some intense material. A "full plate" you might say. But the right people always seem to come along.

    I met a funky artist guy, Tony, at a local coffee shop. He was as sensitive, and as fucked up with relationships at the moment, as I was. We hung out that whole summer. I liked going over to his place because it was away from my answering machine. Yes, it was that far back in technology. I still remember that angst of getting home, seeing if Jenny had called. Stomach in knots either way. I desperately wanted to hear from her, and also was afraid if she did call what she might say.

Hanging out with Tony was interesting. He rented an office space to do his art, but also lived there too, using the communal bathroom down the hall. I loved his free spirit. I loved to nap there too, wake up and go watch him paint. I know that besides my journal, it was friends like him who understood what being on the lower end of the relationship totem pole was like. How we were strong, but yet we could be pulled around so much. Both of us were going through similar situations. Both us kind of fucked up but functional.

My self-torment over Jenny made it hard for me to eat, but one night at the end of the summer, we had dinner with a few friends. Tony saw me eating a veggie burger, and looked at me, confused. Back then, in Kansas, it was not common for someone to be a vegetarian. And all he'd seen me eat for three months were candy bars, pancakes, ice cream—and wine. I had purposely been eating fattening foods because I wanted to make the food count against my weight loss. Tony didn't know I was a vegetarian. We laughed so hard. Sad and happy. We both had tears from crying, realizing how much I'd changed over the summer.

Another friend that helped me through this time in my life was a young girl, Margaret, that I'd met in our file room at work. Oddly enough, she was well older than her actual age, and gave me so much insight into my own life. Margaret was as emotional as I was, and we laughed at how we first met, there in the file room. I'd gone there to cry. She was there already, crying amongst the huge rows of films on rolling shelving. In the following months, we'd meet there a lot.

Margaret was wonderful. I found sanctuary at her family's home. One time I arrived there, disheveled and feeling down. Her mom gave me a shot glass of something and told me to go nap, she'd wake me for dinner. Being an Italian home, sauce was simmering, and the whole house was welcoming and pleasant. Intelligent kids, caring mom and dad. It was what I needed.

I was trying as hard as I could to keep it all together. Leaning on friends when I could, when I needed to. Being at home in my apartment, I felt achingly lonely. At one point, in that fall of 1998, the roommate that I had was not home, but his shotgun was.

I looked it over, trying to figure out how to hold the long gun correctly, with my short arms. Kim hadn't done it right and she had to crawl across the floor and shoot herself again. I would make sure that I would do it right.

But I also knew the anguish of what Kim did to me and to her family, and I didn't want to do that to my family. Because of my journals that I kept, I have my thoughts and actions written down and it's a little startling to see who I was back then, my thought processes, and my whole figuring out process of how to shoot myself properly.

I ended up calling my friend Jason, a psych nurse I had met during a two-week annual training almost ten years before. When I think of someone I can count on, he always comes to mind. Jason talked me down, calmed me enough so that I could put the gun down and go to sleep. For several years after this incident, I would use the same mantra that he offered me. Sitting on a magic carpet, thinking wonderful thoughts about how I can fly. Lifting me up up and away from where I was. Imagining the beautiful sights, sounds, and smells while on that magic carpet ride.

When I woke up in the morning, I called my therapist. I realized that either I had to commit myself or leave Kansas. A coworker had been on lithium and I asked my therapist about the medication. We discussed the pros and cons and I decided that my best alternative was just to get out of there. I felt that if I could change my atmosphere, it could change my thoughts, my attitudes.

It was more than past time to say goodbye to Kansas. I was turning 30 and decided this could be my new start.

From my various all-across-America phone interviews, I knew that I would be able to get a job wherever I wanted to. Not many people were nationally registered in radiology, CT, and also MRI. Plus, I knew how to transcribe, did ultrasound for nine years, fluoroscopy, emergency trauma, and on-call work for eleven years, and mammography for five. I was interim director of the radiology department, too. In Desert Storm, I was the NCOIC (non-commissioned officer in charge) for my X-ray department, even more of a plus since I'd been only 22. I had not taken the Radiology registry until five years after X-ray school, a difficult feat, from a limited military school at that. Six months compared to the civilian two years. One radiologist had told me that I'd never amount to anything. He was so wrong.

I had heard Austin, Texas was a fun city. My old friend, Larry, had moved to Austin a few years before. Although we'd lost touch, I called him out of the blue to tell him I was thinking of moving there. I had three job interviews lined up. I told Larry that if he could find me a great French cafe, fun gay clubs, and indie movie theaters that I liked, I'd move.

Larry showed me his favorite places all over Austin. Some really neat clubs, including one that had a private entrance. It all seemed secretive and fun, like he had shown me an underground part of Austin. Of course all of the food was good. I found out Austin's love of breakfast tacos. And margaritas, and Mexican martinis. The movie theater scene back then was certainly better than it is now. Now it's more corporate. But fortunately back then, we had one theater that was the first of its kind in America—they'd bring you a full menu of food throughout the whole film. And buckets of beer! They also had fun game nights and film festivals where you could get on stage to do wacky things and win prizes.

My first time on that stage was a contest where we volunteers were given a blow-up doll and had to make love to her for ten seconds. (Longer than you'd think.) The first contestants were a couple of guys, doing the usual to the poor doll. Then another female and I were up. The audience preferred the girl and I do the chick together. The MC asked if either of us had made love to a woman before. I said yes and the audience went crazy. Anyway, after seeing the guys go wild with the doll, I did the same and had her in all kinds of positions. The girl and I won. The MC then kept on asking us questions about our boyfriends. It was quite obvious that he did not catch on that I didn't have a boyfriend, but the theater did, laughing at each question.

Anyway, my three job interviews went well. The place that I liked the most liked me. They actually created a position for me. My hard work had paid off. And hopefully luck was now on my side.

I moved to Austin, as was my choice, and started the next journey of my life.

5

Here I was, 30, single, in a new city, and making more money than I had ever made before. I stayed with my friend Larry and his wife Sheri for about a month until I could find my own apartment. I hadn't yet given up my daily-bottle-of-wine habit and I was still smoking a couple packs a day. I started to feel stupid being the only one going outside for a cigarette. Plus, I had some blood clot issues from the combination of birth control pills (for heavy bleeding), smoking, and St. John's Wort (for depression). With a family history of heart problems, I decided it was time to quit smoking. So over the next week, that's what I did. I quit.

How did I do it? I figured out my cigarette triggers—when I liked to smoke. Most often that was post-meal, while writing in my journal, and while having a cup of coffee. And when drinking alcohol. I started out by delaying the cigarette by ten minutes, then stretched it out to twenty minutes, then thirty minutes. If I could go that long, the itch to smoke subsided. I also didn't like going outside alone for a smoke while my friends were inside. Austin had long been a no-smoking-indoors city. I loved that. It made is so much easier for me. At any rate, I quit within one week. Yes, one week. I knew I had to make it happen. It felt so good to be in control of myself in that way. Empowering, for sure. And yet truth be told, I still dream of smoking sometimes. It's weird how it stays with you, decades later.

Austin is a fun town with lots to do outside, and lots to do if you want to party. A lot of partying. The bars on the main street downtown have literal open doors, inviting you in, and live music is playing everywhere. Austin calls itself "The Live Music Capitol of The World." I think they have a lot to offer for live music, especially comparing to the many cities I've traveled.

When I first visited Austin, David and another mutual friend came down here with me. One night we went out, and it was raining hard. We bounced from bar to bar, running in the rainy street, laughing as we jumped over puddles into the open doorways, welcoming us to the drink and the music. During the day, we had the local drink, the margarita. One place had a 2-drink limit. Whew, potent stuff! We were tanked at 2 pm. We picked up a few things at a locally sourced food place for a picnic in the park. We ate and then closed our eyes and napped. Very nice, very needed post-margaritas! The locally sourced food thing was a fairly new concept back then. Austin is the home to a now well-known national chain store that offers "whole foods." I guess they mean not all processed stuff. When I moved here, that store and a few like it, was one of the draws. Being vegetarian was not at all odd here. So yeah, I felt like this could be home.

I met fun people in Austin right away. One invited me to go cycling with her and her friends. I had a bicycle that

I hadn't used much, but I'd brought it with me to Texas anyway so I figured I'd go out with them. As I did my first few rides, I realized that I was amazingly good at it. Those friends noticed too. One of these friends, Frankie, asked me to do a triathlon with her.

"I don't know how to swim," I stated.

Frankie said, "I'll tell you what. I'll teach you how to swim if you teach me how to ride up hills like you do on your bike."

As I hung out more with Frankie, she taught me things about swimming and running. And life. She shared with me that she had dissociative identity disorder (DID). That made so much sense to me! I felt that the person running in front of me was someone different and had longer legs than my short friend, Frankie.

The next time we ran, I yelled out, "Who in the hell are you?"

In a little lower voice, she answered, "Mitchell."

"How tall are you, Mitchell?"

"Just over six feet."

I laughed so hard. Now I knew why I was having trouble keeping up. I ended up straining my leg too, trying to maintain that same stride length. But I became a better runner.

Frankie's multiple personalities also included a bunch of kids inside her and I was pleased to meet a lot of them. They were the ones that showed me how to swim. We sat in the bottom of the pool holding our breaths, having a tea party. It was their way of showing me that it was OK to be calm when you're under the water. I learned a lot from all of those kids.

Connection, Confession, Redemption

Meeting people in Austin was easy. Maybe it was easy for me too when I was in Kansas. When I lived in Kansas, I hung out with some "woo woo" kind of people. I think back then, the gay people, the artists, the people that society did not want to think about, all hung out together. I started to teach myself how to do color therapy (which I still do) and I'd also learned about doing feedback with the body to help make decisions. Any decision. Our bodies know what we need. I still use this body testing on myself and with friends. And I did it with Frankie.

One day at my house, one of the kids inside Frankie said she was allergic to my cat. I wanted to give her some of my homeopathic meds, but was not sure of the dose. (Yes, there was a full grown person in front of me, but the kid inside was the one having the allergy). I did the body testing, for the right dose. The kid's allergy symptoms went away not long after taking the meds. The next day, I asked Frankie about the kids, to get feedback on if what I said or did was right with them, adjusting the dose. It was.

From my time spent with Frankie and the kids, I learned that kids need structure and guidance. And comforting. I also realized that adults are just as scared sometimes, just like a kid. Spending time with these kids helped me in becoming an excellent MRI tech. I tell people that I like to treat all of my patients like they are seven. It works. We all get scared. And we all welcome a calming understanding person. Time with Frankie made me more sensitive to all kinds of people. And that helped me in my career.

Before moving to Austin, I worked at one of the two hospitals in that Kansas college town. After Desert Storm, I figured I could do x-ray all day and night, since during the war, I was dropped feet first into it. At the hospital in those days, everyone did every modality. Within two weeks I learned mammography, sonography, CT, more fluoroscopy. At that time, 1991, we only had a national registry for radiology.

When I went in on weekends to do morning portable imaging, I realized that the transcription was not done until afternoons. So, I learned how to transcribe, too. I'd do the morning portables, and then transcribe from the day before. In the afternoon, I'd do those portable exams, and distribute the imaging reports to the floors. I also liked to organize, so I took over the ordering for our department. Yeah, I like to keep busy and get shit done.

And I like to make the workplace fun. One day I was hanging out in the front office with our transcriptionist, Denise, who was ridiculously funny. The envelopes with the paychecks were on the counter. We were scheming on how to open our boss's check. He was an asshat, and we wanted to see how much he was paid to do nothing. We talked about using a candle to heat up the envelope glue and then laughed so hard, picturing the envelope bursting into flames. Explain THAT to him.

Denise continued the report she'd been working on and I watched her type. The paragraph started with "The CT abdomen and pelvis was acquired in the usual fashion…. and then the kidneys burst into flames!" HAHA! I almost peed my pants, laughing so hard, only able to point at her screen. We laughed harder, thinking about the radiologist who never reviewed his typed-out reports before putting them in the Finished bin. What if he'd been the one to "not review" her flaming kidneys report?! Yeah, it's the little things that make a workplace a fun place. Medical humor at its finest.

Reminds me of another story. (Of course.) One day I was doing an ultrasound on a male patient. Ultrasound techs fill out a worksheet on each patient with organ measurements. Knowing that this same radiologist might get my worksheet and have to read my patient's exam, I decided to be a bit passive aggressive. Or a prankster. I filled out the measurements for the organs, the gallbladder, etc., but also added measurements for ovaries. I got a call a few hours later. "Do. Not. Ever. put down measurements for ovaries on a male patient again." Oh, to be a stupid 23-year-old!

Guys, usually, are fun to image. One night we got a call from the emergency room and they needed assistance. An older guy had gotten a piece of wiring stuck in his penis. Yup. Of course, they tapped the lesbian to image this guy. I decided to use mammography cassettes for finer detail and as I was getting the room set up, I had the guy have a seat on the table. He was only wearing his gown and socks. I stepped out of the room for a minute, to let my coworkers have it. Ha! Actually I went to get my gloves and when I stepped back into the room, he had his gown up, and had just pulled at a piece of wire that was sticking out of his penis, yelling "THERE IT IS! GRAB IT!"

I replied, "NO!"

He pulled it out, bloody wire and all, tossing it in the trash can as he sped out the door and back to the ER. I did not chase him.

In 1993, I was 25, was loving my work, and asked for more things to learn. That January, I'd started to learn nuclear medicine. Both hospitals in town had jointly purchased an MRI scanner together and about a month after starting nuclear medicine, my administrator asked me to go to the other hospital, where the MRI was located, to be our representative MRI tech. Within the first six months, though, I said I was going to quit going there. I figured out that the two guys "teaching me" MRI were doing their best to not teach me. I'd struggled with learning the modality, as there was a lot of confusion between what they told me to do and what the radiologists said I should do. The radiologists often kicked back exams that I'd done, seeing errors. I realized the dudes at the other hospital were screwing me over. I thought at the time that it was because I was from the opposing hospital. But now that I think about military jobs with men, and the past three decades of imaging with men, I can also attribute this push to not teach me to another reason. I was a woman. Plus, I was a lesbian.

A lot of men, more so back then, felt threatened or intimidated by a lesbian. A lesbian is like an alien to them, someone they have no control over, and have no chance of sleeping with. They don't know how to relate to a woman that is their age/demographic, but won't have sex with men. If you think it's not true, shut it. Walk in my shoes for a day and maybe you'll get it. And don't get me started on male-female pay equality. I know for a fact that I've made less, in the same position, as male counterparts. That's bullshit. F'in bullshit. But I digress. (And I will again and again.)

Anyway, back to my story about the two guys who thought they could mess with me. I had support from my supervisor. I found, for the first time really, that I was valued.

Connection, Confession, Redemption

Within two weeks, my hospital administrator asked me to go back, that the issue had been taken care of. They probably took care of it so fast because our hospital was losing out on the profits of having us get credit for some of the MRIs. But I did see how I was being respected by my hospital. And that felt good. At any rate, only one guy remained, to teach me. He showed me things that were directly opposite of what he and the other tech had been showing me for half a year. It was an eye opening experience. I learned that I needed to do my best to stand up for myself. And I found that money talks. In a business of patient care for profit, it never hurts to think of the administration's view of things.

I finally got properly trained. And I got the last laugh. Within a few months, I was the only one doing MRI. I was still doing part time x-ray, ultrasound, and intermittent CT. And now MRI. A few months later, I got a new MRI partner. He was very fun, very funny, and made the job a blast.

Back then, MRI took so long that sometimes I had time to go for a cigarette while one set of images was reconstructing. Fact is, I loved to multitask, then and now. One time scanning an MRI patient, while that was running, I went and did an ultrasound. I like to keep busy!

The job had its funny, not funny moments. One time I was doing a cervical spine MRI on a patient. The coil for that particular scanner was quite large, covering the head, down to the upper chest. I left to grab a smoke. When I came back, the scanner was still going, but it was empty. I almost shit my pants. I peeked into the scan room window, around the corner. The guy was getting dressed (the scanners were very low-powered back then, so the patients could put stuff on the counter, including wallets, etc.). I stopped the scanner, opened the scan room door, and said, "Hey, how are ya!?"

The guy said, "I had to get out. I'm done. I scooted down the table and got out."

Doing MRI, it is not uncommon for a patient to stop midway. For various reasons. Pain, claustrophobia (like this guy), or whatever reason they give me. The radiologist then looks at whatever we can give them. If they feel they have enough to generate a report for the referring physician, then they will. If not, the patient is asked to come back. Back then, we did not have anyone to help the patient, just us MRI techs. Now there is a radiology nurse that specializes in giving pain management and whatnot needed for certain exams. The need for these nurses to assist in MRI procedures has increased. The guy who slipped out of the scanner due to claustrophobia could have had some sedation help via the nurse.

Partial scans are not the norm, and having the patient scoot out of the machine is not the norm, but I have done all kinds of scans I never imagined. I have imaged animals for Kansas State University—dogs, cats, and horse legs. Yes, just the legs, for pathology. Anyway, I enjoyed my work, and as always, making it fun whenever I could. One day walking out of the hospital after a long and tiring shift, I headed to my car in the parking lot which faced a coliseum. A huge roar came from across the street as the football crowd at the stadium cheered. I immediately put my arms in the air, giving myself a huzzah at a job well done, thanking the crowd for their enthusiastic response to my work.

I liked the challenges of the fairly new modality that was MRI. Not much was known about MRI, the process, the applications. Our local ear, nose, and throat doctor asked the radiologists about imaging temporal mandibular joints (TMJ). The radiologists said MRI did not image that small part of the body. I decided to try anyway. I put one of the small body parts coils on the MRI table. I started a sequence of images that was long in duration, not specific to certain anatomy. I jumped on the table, centering the side of my head, where my TMJ was at. I was able to then go back to the scanner, line up sets of images to the anatomy I saw on the screen. From there, I carefully crawled back into the scanner, letting the small parts coil get each set of new images. I showed this to the radiologists, and amazed, they pulled together a protocol for imaging the TMJ.

Neat thing, I was the first imaging tech to work at both hospitals at the same time. I was also interim director for a few months, before I left in 1998. When I left, they had to hire TWO people to replace the jobs I was doing.

I remember being both pissed off and proud about that fact. And thrilled to be going to Austin.

6

Okay, let's skip to four years later. Austin is great and I switched jobs, joining the imaging company that I'd be with for the next two decades. I had been doing weekend work for them, but a day position opened up. 6:30am–2pm-ish. Perfect! I also was at the end of a four-year relationship. Dakota and I had had a good time getting to know each other. We traveled to Italy, traveled to each other's hometowns. We will always have a good bond. Now it was time for us to move on. No hard feelings. We had done some good work towards the end, working on relationship communication. I learned a lot about applying this to any kind of relationship. "Mirroring" was a big thing I've learned. When I can repeat back what the other person is trying to say, they know that I am actually listening. It's important! I also learned a lot about house stuff, and I learned about myself, too. I not only love the work, but am very good at drywalling, painting trim and walls, and doing brick/paving work.

When I was getting ready to leave that house and Dakota, I, as usual, found another woman to be with. No, she was not under some rock, like I suddenly "found" her. LOL. I still was doing like I'd been doing all of my life...not being single for too long. This new woman and I dated for about a year. She was interesting. Totally woo woo. Cajun, involved in mystical type stuff. During that year, we went to a non-denominational church that offered some fascinating classes. One was "Introduction to Animal Communication."

The participants brought pictures of their pets, no other information, and shared each picture with others in the group. Looking at a picture of an animal I did not know anything about, including the owner, I centered my mind, and listened/felt what came to me. Wow, I found I was really good at it. I got SO much right about that pet, and also about the human attached to them. Seriously, I was able to know characteristics of that human, too. I started doing animal communication sessions, for donation only. Maybe I could have made my livelihood from it, who knows, but I did it because it felt right to do it. And I've been told I'm so f'in good at it.

I also worked more on color therapy. Knowing that blue is a healing/cooling color, I tried it once on my ankle after hitting the shit out of it on a wheelbarrow. (You know how that feels, right?) Anyway, holy fuckamoly, eleven minutes after I'd hit it, it was already turning YELLOW. Like, healing. Alright. Damn straight. Yeah, this works!

Color therapy. Animal communication. MRI and hospital work. Fixing houses. Running and biking. So many choices and interests. Career options. But fear stops me, (stops most of us), from pursuing different passions. I've been working on that fear for a long time. It's stopped me from doing part-time MRI work and part-time animal communication/color therapy. I've been told over and over from Reiki masters, psychics, and animal communicators that either I was more powerful than they were, or just so damn good that there was no reason for me to need THEM. And I know it, but still I hold back.

There's a guy in Austin that is known for his psychic abilities. Readings, classes, he does it all. I went to him once to help me find my mom's birth father. He wondered why I was even there. He said I know as much as he does. It makes me think, as I write this. I have so many more things that I can do, that I can accomplish, with this brain. I get sidetracked though. I get fearful of the abilities I have.

I know, and I've shown myself and others, what I am able to do. If I calm my mind down and focus, I know I could bring in loved ones that have passed. Just like the psychic. I know it.

But do I pursue it?

As for animal communication, yes. I love animals more than I love humans. They are SO freakin' funny. I giggle, we giggle. I cry, too. A co-worker, Jon, had some alpaca. One adult female that he'd just gotten was very sad. Jon asked me to talk to her, to communicate and find out the problem. I did. She was sooooo sad, missing her baby. The mama alpaca showed me a large field, high grass, and her baby. She missed her baby, as she had been taken away from it. At Jon's farm now where she was, there was a baby alpaca, and she cared for it like it was hers. I told Jon what the alpaca had said and shown me. Jon's jaw dropped. He said that he'd just pulled her from Colorado, and yes, she'd recently given birth. (Who the fuck even does that?! Taking a mama from her newborn?!) Jon knew she was already taking care of a little one on his farm. He felt horrible. So yeah, I talked to her again, letting her know that her human felt horrible, and that even though she missed her baby in Colorado, there was a baby here that needed her. She felt a lot better, relieved to be able to help here. Jon gave me an update a few days later that the mama alpaca was, in fact, lighter in her step, happier. This is one of many animal stories.

A funny one, and a WTF moment, comes to mind. I was getting tutored in Algebra (yes, at age 36. I was doing online classes in Business Management). The tutor had a bunch of pets. Birds, mice, snakes. As I walked by, one of the mice grabbed my attention. Hey there, sad, sad, hey, hey!! I told the guy that the mouse was sad. He said he'd noticed that the mouse hid a lot. I calmed my mind, and tuned in, and listened to the mouse. The mouse told me, "I'm in this damn hallway, and the cage across from me has a snake in it. It wants to eat me, I'm scared."

It was so freakin' obvious. I told the guy, who now looked at each cage, scratching his head and said, "Yeah-hhh, I can see that now. I guess I'll separate them." Doh.

My favorite thing to do is to help a human with their pet's process of passing on. Like pet hospice. My friend Michelle asked me to talk to her dog, Reba, who was in failing health. Reba was not doing well, and Michelle hoped that I could help with their communication. Michelle wanted to do absolutely everything she could to help Reba be as comfortable and happy as possible in the time she had left. I got to know Reba, what she liked, did not like, and what she most needed. Michelle was grateful to give Reba what she needed, and they both were able to handle the end much easier. It's special for me, being able to help both pet and person.

My ex Dakota had two beautiful dogs and called one day after our breakup to ask about Gator, who seemed to have an upset stomach. I went and talked to Gator. He said there was something he'd eaten, like a large acorn. I was skeptical because the dogs had no acorns near them. They were in a double gated area where there was no access to any kind of trees with acorns. I told Dakota what Gator had said. Right away, she said, yes, it's possible. There were some neighborhood kids who'd been throwing magnolia tree seed pods at the dogs' pen. (Asshats.) Gator had eaten one of those seed pods.

A couple of years later, Dakota called to tell me that Gator was lethargic, and she was super sad, worried about him. I checked on Gator, and he showed me his upper neck, base of the skull. He had something there, and that was it. Done, he was done for. I told Dakota this, crying. She took him in to the vet. They confirmed a brain tumor. After Gator had passed on, I checked on him. OMG, he was how I remembered him when I lived with him. Jumping, jumping, happy happy, jumping up and down like a baby goat. It felt so good to tell Dakota how well Gator was doing.

My friend Brenda has an awesome cat named Dexter. I checked on him one day, and he said he was "dry." Dry skin, dry hair, dry other parts of his body, but not dry bones. Recent. I asked Brenda if she'd changed anything recently. She said she'd run out of his usual food and subbed another food in that line. Yup, it did not work as well with Dexter. I asked Dexter how long it would take to fix. I got the numbers 4 and 7. We figured out that four days is the time that he'd start to be better with added eggs and tuna. Seven days, he'd be back on track with his old food added in, replacing his food he'd not done well with. I love helping! I could tell stories about animals all day.

Helping the pet's human facilitate a peaceful, meaningful journey brings me so much joy. I know that the humans can feel helpless when their pets are in need. Knowing that they can help their pet is wonderful. It's also deeply meaningful for me getting information once the pet has passed on. I love sharing that information. The pet is SO much happier (most of the time).

So, yeah, I guess it's obvious that I love animals. Their humor, their love for life, their carefree way that they love. Man, if we all could be like that.

7

After the Cajun relationship, I decided to write down a list of what I wanted in a life partner. I'd had experiences in the past with the power of positive thoughts, of sharing positivity, and receiving positive stuff back. I knew that putting thoughts and ideas out there would send out those vibrational frequencies, thoughts of what I wanted, and I would attract back those things.

Here's the list that I wrote down, in the order of importance to me for my life partner:

Sense of humor
Acknowledgement of feelings
Financially responsible
Likes job
Comfortable sexually
Comfortable spiritually
Likes to travel
Likes to exercise
Likes to eat/have drinks
Good talker/listener
Knowledgeable in books/music/art/etc.
Can compromise

Supportive
Neat without being anal (towards me)
Likes their family
Likes breakfast in bed
Romantic
Long walks while talking
Drinks coffee on a hot day
Will leave me a note or a message that I was thought of
Will take a bath with me
Will draw a bath w/music, candles, wine/beer for me
Likes to be in the rain, especially kissing

When I first moved to Austin, I worked at that small imaging company, a place with about ten employees. There was an ultrasound tech that worked there named Cindy that exuded confidence and I would come to see that she was the best ultrasound tech I'd ever meet. You've also just met my wife.

I knew she was gay when I met her. I was surprised to find that she was married. She was super nice to me, overly nice. She left me notes on my bicycle to "be careful on your way home" and gave me sweets or coffee from Starbucks. We all kind of laughed about it at the office, but I knew that she was like a pre-pubescent boy, not sure of what he was doing or why. She'd also do shit to piss me off, like take down my Christmas lights in my MRI area. When I found out it was her, I marched to her ultrasound room and told her to stay out of my area. Later she said she would do anything to get my attention, even if it pissed me off.

I will admit, I also did stuff to get her goat. Cindy has OCD about being neat, and I'd go into her ultrasound (sono) room, and move something a smidge. Like swap one of her Tori Amos CDs, or turn the nozzle on her lotion bottle. She'd come back to the MRI area when this happened, and direct her agitation towards me, knowing it had to be me doing that stuff. Yes, she ticked the box about being neat, but was not judgy towards me as far as neatness went.

We talked about sports, and I told her about my triathlons, rock climbing, and long distance cycling. She also loved to work out, and asked me to come work out at her home gym. I started going to her intimidatingly large home, but did it to find out more about this interestingly complex woman.

I told her about how I did this "women in the outdoors" thing once, with some friends. We did kayaking, learned about tracking animals, and archery. I told her how much fun the archery was, and that I did pretty well. Yeah, I was bragging, trying to impress her. Cindy replied that a few years back, she'd done some archery too. She casually stated that she'd had a representative from Browning ask her to shoot for them. Damn! I felt about an inch tall. LOL.

Cindy loved her job, loved hot coffee on a hot day, loved to exercise, was very neat, liked to leave notes. You see where I am going with this. When I met her husband, I knew he was gay. They'd been childhood sweethearts, and met up again later in life, decided to get married. I've seen that many times with rural gay folk. Sad, really. There was no reason for them to get married, or stay married, but it's common when people are not accepted to be who they are.

But society is getting better. I hope.

Anyway, I realized that in past relationships, I was always with someone that I thought needed my support, my help, or that I thought needed fixing. This wonderful woman asked about me working out at her place, her making me dinner (loves to eat healthy food, but also loves to indulge), all while driving me to and from her house. I decided to let her do it. For once, I let someone take care of ME. I let myself be cared for. Yes, she drew baths for me, left me rose petals, loved long walks, talks, and rainy days. She had traveled a lot, but not so much overseas yet. That was her passion. That, and art, books, history. The best part? She was funnier than shit.

I did have to learn to be taken care of, as this was all new to me. I learned that I deserved love. I found that in the past, I'd made my partners pissed off, not realizing I was doing it on purpose. Enough to make them cry. A lot. And finally, I'd leave, as I always did.

I said something to Cindy once, this strong Marine. And she cried. I was like, oh fuck, I've really messed this up. I realized then that I was the problem. I'd made these women cry. This woman was incredible, and she was worth it, and I needed to calm down. I needed to make this right. I needed to do better. I had found the ONE. She's good at talking, at compromising, and making it work. Heck, Cindy moved into my 700sq ft apartment, and no one killed each other. We loved being that close.

Yes, she ticked all of the boxes on my life partner list. We've now traveled the US, and the world together. We are "those" people who laugh at the wrong parts in the movie theatre. We might keep you up if you stay at our home because we are laughing at something stupid. I know if something happened to us, my family would choose her. Kidding, not kidding! She sends flowers just because. I make sure I vacuum twice a week, keeping my OCD honey happy.

Desiree B.

As I type this, we just passed our 15-year anniversary. We also, on the same day, celebrated our 5th wedding anniversary. We got married in New York City, at Belvedere Castle in Central Park. Our marriage is not difficult. We've not "worked so hard to get where we are" that so many couples state on their anniversary. As a matter of fact, we hashed it out at the beginning, before we had put time in.

Cindy said that before she'd sleep with me, I'd need to give her a blood test, and also a credit report. Yeah. Really. But you know, that's smart. Also smart was the fact that we talked about our spiritual selves, what path we were on. We both know now that we've grown together on this, rather than apart. It's important. We also talked about kids. She'd wanted kids in the past, but decided against it a few years before we'd met. I thought I still wanted kids. I'd tried when I was younger, but was unsuccessful. We did not want to have kids late in life. (We were both 36 when we met, and figured we'd have one at 40 if we did). She said she'd rather travel. I agreed. I knew, once again, that she was the one. I told Cindy that I'd rather go through this life without children if it meant being with her. The pull of seeing a little Desi around did not compare to the whole feeling I had when I was with Cindy.

When it's right, you just know it. So yeah, I got the blood test, and gave her the credit report. I gave them to her on my terms, not on hers. ;)

8

Getting together later in life, (36 was by no means old, but you get to experience relationship ins and outs), Cindy and I wanted to make sure our major paths in life would be at least congruent. One area of importance for both of us was spirituality. Not religion, but spirituality.

When I was a kid, we stopped going to our Lutheran Church when I was about six. My stepdad, Bob, said that the church was becoming too commercial. We lived in a farming community, and the members mainly talked about what new tractor they had purchased, but not about church. Bob stopped taking the family to church, and did not continue any schooling at home. So to say that my knowledge of religion was limited is not overstating it.

In the following years, as I heard about "homosexuals going to Hell" and all of that, I had no plans to learn about ridiculous religion. I also shied away from people that followed any kind of dogma.

It got worse when I moved to Kansas, which is part of the Bible Belt, where religion and politics are beautifully (insert sarcasm) influenced by each other. Not that the US was founded by people who wanted to separate Church and State...ugh.

Connection, Confession, Redemption

I moved to Kansas when I was nineteen, right after Army X-ray school. Since I was so young, my growing up into adulthood happened there, in Kansas. People did some hateful things in the name of religion in that area. Fred Phelps (the anti-gay minister in Topeka looking for nationwide fame) and his whole clan (a bunch of assholes) picketed all kinds of gatherings. College graduations, funerals. They carried signs about how your loved one is dead because somehow they accepted gay people. Complete and total bullshit. I drove by once where they were gathering, and I flipped Fred off. Childish, and probably pointless to a jerk like him, but it felt great!

Many random incidents clued me in that being gay was not welcome there. One beautiful fall day, a friend and I walked along the outskirts of a nice park, chatting. Like people do. Some college dudes drove by and threw trash at us, yelling "fucking lesbians."

Nice.

Sue and I lived in a house with two gay guys. The neighbors were not friendly or welcoming. The couple next door were building a deck. Mysteriously, every day when we came home, pieces of trash wood, and pieces of coconut (they ate a lot of raw coconuts), were thrown on our lawn. Other crap also was always tossed in our yard. The name calling under their breath whenever we arrived home and left for the day sucked, too. We ended up leaving that house.

When I was twenty-five, I dated a Catholic woman who had a hard time with being gay and Catholic. Having to live with what the church said, compared to what she felt about being accepted by God, messed her up. She started going to a non-denominational church. I went with her a few times, wanting to learn some things. I also wanted to see where she was coming from. I thought maybe I could help her let go of some of her issues. We only dated for a year. Part of the end of our relationship was her struggling so much with the contradiction of the peace that the church taught versus how church people actually treated her. Other people's interpretation of the Bible gets pretty whacked.

After we split up, I went to a Lutheran church for a few months with some gay friends. That church had just made a public advertisement that they wanted to accept all people. That seemed fine, but my friends knew so much more about what the pastor was saying than I did. I felt lost most of the time. But we weren't banished for being gay.

I had a coworker, Nan, who was very religious, as was her husband. Nan wanted me to repent or whatever, but wasn't the usual asshole type telling me to do that. So I actually asked her and her husband to give me Bible tutoring. Yes, my brain never can get enough stimulation! Tutoring with them was fine, and I had a few sessions. To me, it was like hearing a children's story. A story, like any children's fable. But a story that most of the world believed, prayed to, killed for, used against one another. The whole religion thing? Not worth it. I did not believe in God anyway; who was I trying to learn about the Bible for? Why was I trying to believe in this fairy tale?

Another nail in the coffin in my quest to learn about religion occurred when I made friends with my physical therapist. Charles was a super nice guy, loved his church, and he talked to me about it sometimes during my PT for my wrist. We agreed to get together sometime, away from work and physical therapy, to hang out and talk. One day, Charles came by my house. He said that it was nice to get to know me as a patient and also as a fellow hospital worker, BUT he would not have any more contact with me, since I was gay. He said it was against the Bible. Me being gay? Him being friends with me because I was a lesbian? It was one more thing to seal the deal on why would I try to believe in some "being" who would teach people to act like this. No thanks. And when my ex, Kim, killed herself, one main reason was that her parents could not take her being gay. Her father had abused her, yet had the balls to condemn her for being gay. Cherry pickers, hypocrites.

Anyway, a few years later, I was maybe 32, and wondering if there really was a God. I thought about it a lot. Like, how can so many people of all walks of life believe in a higher power of some kind, if there is not some truth to it? I was getting therapy from a friend, K, who does this thing called "Bodytalk." Look it up, it's good stuff. Kind of like that thing I did with my friend Frankie, asking her body how much of the sinus meds to give, but a shit ton more in depth. Spiritual, physical, metabolic, all systems of the body, K can tap into it, see where things need to be uncovered, cleaned up. She can help where stuff is being harbored in your body. I went to her, trying to figure out some physical stuff, my wrist, trying to release things. More than that happened.

One time I woke up after falling asleep during a session. I was dreaming, but not dreaming. I saw her. I saw K, her eyes, and I knew it was her, but we were in some village hut. She was a healer, and it was a LONG time ago, like Egyptian time. I also knew that she had been a healer through many lifetimes. I told K this, and she loved it, knowing that yes, she'd been a healer for a long time.

Another time I woke up there, K had already left the room. I looked over at her shelf, at the photo of her former husband who had died before she moved to Texas. I looked at him, with my mind open and calm. He spoke and said, "Tell K that yes, she should buy the shoes."

I was confused, because I didn't remember that I'd talked to anyone that had passed, but more odd, he sounded like Mike Tyson. K and her husband had done theatre together, and I was wondering how he could, with that voice. Did he do comedy? Anyway, I headed down the stairs to find K.

"I think I just talked to your husband."

She cocked her head, quizzically.

"First of all, his voice," I said.

K giggled.

"Did he have a high voice?"

Laughing, she replied, "Yes, it was like Mike Tyson."

Holy crap, yeah.

"He said for you to buy the shoes."

She was incredulous. "Check this out!" K opened the closet, pulling out a pair of old beat up shoes that needed to be replaced. "I've been thinking of getting a new pair, but did not want to spend the money!"

"Well, he says, "Go for it!" I laughed as I was saying it. We both laughed, ecstatic over what had happened.

Another Bodytalk therapy day, as she's working, listening to my body, K casually tells me, "You know, there really IS a God."

I had never mentioned my questions about God. So I was freaked out in a good way that she could feel the questions in my body, and that she wanted to confirm the existence of a God.

Same timeframe, I was at work. I always got there early, to journal, have coffee, before most of my co-workers got in. I was journaling about my God question, does he even hear me. A co-worker came in, said good morning, then poked his head back in and, said, "I was doing my morning meditation, and God told me, "Tell Desiree that yes he hears you.""

I was in shock. I must have looked like a guppy, mouth hanging open. About a month later, I was at my chiropractor's office, sitting in the waiting room. All the sudden, I had this realization, this feeling came over my whole body, like a chemical reaction. I started shaking, crying, sweating, realizing that God was real. The thought of "Footprints in the sand" was real. I suddenly saw all of these moments in my life where I was not really alone. The doc came to get me, and I was still all sweaty, tears down my face. I gave her a quick explanation for my disheveled state, that I'd just had the realization that God was real! She laughed, and said, "Of course God is real!"

Ever since that all happened, I've been enjoying when something happens to validate the existence of God. In 2006, I had a bicycling accident. When I got back to my vehicle, I said, "Thank you, God," out of habit. I got a wash of silver over my body, and a voice saying, "You're welcome."

I knew it was real, but of course still did not believe it, so I said it again. And the voice came humorously yet lovingly back at me. "You're welcome. Smile."

When I got home, I was in our bathroom, cleaning up from the ride. My eye caught the Avon figurines perfume bottles on our shelf. Grandma had given them to Mom, Mom gave to me. I did a double take at them. I had a clear and instant knowing that it was also Grandma with me when I had the accident. I thanked her for being with me. For being one of my angels.

Another time, I was driving, almost to a railroad crossing that I'd gone over nearly every day, mindlessly. "STOP!!!!!!!" was yelled in the car. I hit the brakes. Only a few milliseconds later, a train blew through. That voice saved me from being flattened.

So many stories and instances like this. These things are around, all the time. We, rather, I, need to pay attention. But you know what? Again fear stops me. Not a fear of God. For God is love. Fear stops me from being comfortable with "knowing stuff." I think it's the fear of what others think. Of me. Even as I write this, I wonder about the feedback, the blowback, from those people who are not believers in things that I have discussed here and am passionate about.

Well, I guess we'll see.

9

I feel the need to back up a little and expand on what it's like to be gay. Yes, I've said a little, but there's more. Way more. I want you to have a tiny clue what gay people go through every day. At least what it's like outside of open places like Austin.

There does not need to be any specific incident to let you know that gay people are treated like shit most of the time. It has gotten a lot better, but in Kansas in the 80's and 90's, not so great. At work related get-togethers, straight people could talk about their boyfriend or girlfriend, but if you were gay, no way. I had to say "partner" or "roommate." It was like they wanted to pretend I was a heterosexual and that my partner was not a "she." I got tired of saying "they/them" instead of saying "she" or "her." For example: "Yeah, my roommate and I went on a cruise. They had not been on a cruise before."

If a co-worker asked about me seeing someone, the expected reply was "Yeah, I have someone." Nothing more. No names. No information. Stupid. God forbid, I talk the way straight people talk. When coworkers chatted around the water cooler about their home life, no one wanted to

Connection, Confession, Redemption

hear about mine. For fuck's sake, they mentioned their boyfriend's actions in bed. How does my saying something cute my girlfriend did warrant an ugly scowling face as a reply compared to that?

A couple years after I'd started working at the hospital, I began talking about my girlfriend, like everyone else did about their partners and spouses. I wanted to talk about my life with coworkers, about the same things that they talked about. Having a romantic dinner is not only for straight people, and I have a right to talk about my date the same as anyone else. I started talking about my own life. Because my life was as normal to me as theirs was to them.

If they made a big deal out of me mentioning my girlfriend, then it was THEIR issue.

I'd say something like "My girlfriend and I took a boat out this weekend," and if someone would ask "Did you and your friend get a sunburn?" I'd correct them casually. "No, luckily we didn't, my girlfriend is good about bringing the sunscreen." Conversations like that.

Even now, I am married, yet some people, including some family, and for sure some ultra conservative people in online clubs we belong to, still refer to my wife as my friend. They know who she is. My wife. That attitude, that treatment is so disrespectful. Some people are assholes.

As time went on, my coworkers became more comfortable with me talking, and the couple of people that did not were treated a bit differently. Those people became the odd person out.

Being gay is normal. I always knew I was gay. I told myself I was gay, out loud, when I was 16. I'd known if for as long as I can remember. I had a crush on my 1st grade teacher, so for sure a long time. But I never said anything to my family.

When I got home from Xray school, my mom had found a letter that my girlfriend had written me. Mom was pissed at first. Then she wondered if she'd done something wrong as a mother. I have found a lot of family and friends react that way. They feel like now they have to live with having a gay family member, how are they going to explain that. Now they have to change their life for the gay person. More often than not, they make it about themselves, and not the actual person who is gay.

Mom had a bunch of emotions that turned inward. We talked about it, and she was able to see I was always this way. It was just how I was born. Nothing to do with how Mom raised me.

I've talked to coworkers and friends about how my mom eventually became one of those "PFLAG" advocates: "Parents and family of lesbians and gays." Mom will shoot someone down in a conversation if they talk badly about a gay person. She proudly says, "My daughter is a lesbian, and she's been through a lot. I love her for standing up for herself." That kind of thing.

An older coworker, Helen, was religious, and also loving and open to talking about most things. I happened to know, from seeing a photo of her son, that he was gay. She did not talk about it, to him, to anyone. She seemed to not acknowledge it. Helen referred to him and his "friends" the same way that people expected me to refer to mine.

One day, Helen pulled me aside, asking to talk with me. I knew what the conversation was going to be about. I also I knew that this was the reason I was vocal about being gay, and also about gay rights. Helen said her son had just came out to her. She said as a mother, she felt guilt about anything she might have done. She also felt anger at the situation. She remembered what I'd said about my own mom. With that, before she replied back to him, before she sat down with him, she calmly went through the realistic aspects of it all. Helen said to him what my mom had said to others about me. That she loved him, that God made him that way, and she would always love him.

Yet, there are still so many families who shun their gay children. It's pathetic.

I have friends who wonder why I will have a rainbow flag somewhere, or why I advocate Pride parades. "Keep it to yourself, it is no one else's business" even some gay friends will say. Well hell. When I joined the military, I had to literally sign some bullshit questions like "I have not had any homosexual thoughts." And "I do not intend to engage in any homosexual behavior." I felt so torn about it. I wanted to serve my country, but I didn't understand what that had to do with being gay.

Luckily, the military entrance paperwork has changed. I even welcomed "Don't Ask, Don't Tell" in 1993. It became illegal to ask a service member if they were a homosexual. But it also meant that you still had to stay in the closet. It was not enough, but damn, it was progress. You may not agree, but this is my damn opinion.

Until 2011, I still could not visit my life partner in the hospital. I was not "family." Some straight person could say that was their wife or whatever. No proof was needed. Me? Forget it. THAT is why I advocate rainbows, and parades. To promote awareness. That we are not just a small group of people. We are everywhere. We should have the same governmental rights and human rights as straight people. There are also a lot of local community care groups and national groups that march during these parades, promoting awareness. It's important.

In 2015, the Supreme Court struck down all bans on gay marriage. We were allowed to get married, legally, in our home state of Texas. I wanted to make sure that if something happened to me, my family would not have to deal with my medical needs and decisions. My wife should be the one to do that. Filing as a Civil Partner does not guarantee the same rights that a husband or wife does. It is also not the same as a legal power of attorney. A lot of people do not realize that.

I will always remember the day of the announcement. I was at home, with the TV on in the living room, but was in the back of the house, in the workout room. I heard some breaking news come on, that the Supreme Court had ruled that marriage was legal in all states. I went out to the TV, and stared at it. My phone rang in the kitchen, it was Mom. Back then, she never called during the day unless it was urgent. I answered the phone, crying, saying "Is it really real?"

Mom was crying too. "Yes, it's really real!" It was so wonderful to hear that from my own mother. I know for a fact that there are so many who will never ever have that kind of support from their parents.

I know, I know, this section, this talk of gay stuff is long, but I gotta write it. It's not WHO I am, but damn, it has affected my life. You know, when I got married, my employer informed me that my wife would get an insurance policy. For free. So there is this secret club, stuff THEY got. Married people. Tax relief. This makes it not Church only, but Church and State.

People who say this shit should be left in private have obviously not had anything denied them, or taken away from them. Wake up.

I had a family member who said she could not go to my wedding, because in the Bible it says that marriage is between a man and a woman, and for procreation only. I immediately replied, "So when you married your husband, neither of you were at the age to have children anymore; how is this different than mine?"

She hung up on me.

I guess getting your beliefs shaken up a little, or rather questioned, does not make people comfortable. Well, you can live in your little comfortable bubble, your glass house, and try to throw stones.

There have been some wonderful people in my family, too. When Mom told the whole family that I was gay, most of my siblings initially freaked, but my oldest brother, Victor, did not. He read all he could on gay people and he and his wife took his family to the Minneapolis Pride Festival. He wanted to make sure their kids were well rounded, could see other people's views, other walks of life. He said he wanted to understand his sister better. He wanted his kids to understand their aunt better. Me! I was astounded at that kind of love, for not just the gay community, but for me.

So, yeah, I am gonna keep on flying my flag. Thanks for listening.

10

I didn't know much about my dad. Or rather I never met him. Life is messy. There's no blame, there's just a bunch of sticky relationships that happen to every one of us. Whether we see them as sticky or not. Sometimes you think it's straightforward, but it might not seem that way to others involved. For example, it may seem straightforward that a relationship didn't work out, but when a child was born from that relationship, it's not only about those two people. The parents go their separate ways for whatever reasons. But that child may want to know more about their parents and grandparents. I think it's important to keep contact somehow. That's my two cents anyway. Maybe knowing my dad might have soothed me in some way as a kid.

But that's life. My mom has told me his name and some stuff, and that I look like him. I guess my dad left town right after I was born. Mom went to his trailer to show me to him. He nodded and said thanks, and he closed the door. Then he disappeared.

Of course, I didn't know that when I was a kid. That's pretty harsh to handle. And obviously, Mom was better off without him. But knowing I didn't have the same dad as my siblings rocked me.

What I did know about him when I was younger, I honestly don't remember. I think part of the reason I am writing this book is to preserve some of my memories. There is so much shit I do not remember. There are many things I don't remember that you'd think I would. It's not just menopause memory issues. I have a huge block of things that I have no recollection of. There's a lot of us that were in Desert Storm that were exposed to Sarin gas, treatments beforehand, and treatments during that have some similar memory issues. So there's that. But....

Anyway....

In November 1990, when our Army Reserve unit was activated for Desert Storm, I was not surprised. The unit that I was in didn't make much money. Or rather, we were not funded well. When we traveled for our annual trainings, we went by the bus load, as flying was too expensive. Two years prior to Desert Storm, we made an expensive trek down to Brooke Army Medical Center in San Antonio for us to work in hospitals. I guess to hone our skills. The next year we went to Camp Shelby Army Reserve base in Hattiesburg, Mississippi. It's one of the largest mobilization stations of the US Armed Forces command. We spent the next two weeks putting up and tearing down our EVAC hospital there. Think of the TV show M.A.S.H. That's what our hospital was like. Anyway, they were getting us ready. And we got activated for Desert Storm.

At Fort Riley, on a cold assed morning, I was in formation. I was handed a letter, from an old friend of my mom's, a lady who also knew my dad. I think she was the person that actually introduced them. I didn't know what the letter was about, so I ripped it open it while I was standing there, happy to get mail.

She had written to give me my father's address and phone number. Maybe it was because I had been sent to war, or maybe she just found out where he was or maybe she had just learned that I had been trying to locate him. Doesn't matter. Here was his name staring at me, and his contact information. So many emotions went through me. My legs felt weak. He was a person that now really existed in the world, and not just in my head. I had tried to imagine meeting my birth father forever, but now suddenly he had more substance to him.

First chance I got, I called him. I cannot tell you why, but I do not remember much about the call. I think it's because it was so normal. Nothing earth-shaking. It was a normal conversation. No "Wow, it's really you, my daughter!!" Nothing like that. It was a conversation between two people that obviously had a connection, but no past, no history to talk about. And no future. No declarations of love. He was polite and gave me any information that I asked for, but no admission of paternity or that he was interested in meeting me. We had a decent chat, and that was that. It felt flat. I called him a few more times. He always ended up saying that he still didn't think I was his daughter. It was both painful, and frustrating.

I had craved information my whole life. I hired a guy to do some investigative work for me. We did not have internet like we do today, so I needed help. I wanted information about my birth father, and if I had siblings from him. The guy found a list of names of people who were at the same address, also some others who were at different addresses together. That was it. No real clue as to who were my possible siblings and who weren't. The investigator only provided information. I had to piece together the puzzle.

There was a boy named Jeffrey on the list that was born six years after I was. I was pretty sure that this boy Jeffery was my little brother. Being the youngest of five when I was growing up, it was exciting to think that I had a younger sibling. I'd heard that I looked a whole lot like my dad. I thought it would be great to see what my little brother looked like. At any rate, one of the times I called my father, a young man answered the phone. I asked for LeRoy, my birth father, and was told he wasn't in. And then I bit the bullet and went in.

"Is your name Jeff?"

"Yes."

I said, "Hello, this is Desiree, your sister."

He seemed a little surprised, but not very. I decided to continue on.

"How old are you?" I asked.

"Sixteen."

This boy and I proceeded to talk about things such as what he looks like, things that he liked to do. I know that this was not a usual conversation that a stranger and a 16-year-old boy would have. I knew we weren't strangers though. It would be several years later that my gut feeling was confirmed, and that later on I would affectionately call him my big little brother, and he'd call me his little big sister. (He's 6'5 and I'm 5'3.)

In 1998, on a road trip with some friends, knowing that I would be passing through the city LeRoy lived in, I called his house. I wanted to ask if I could look at him face-to-face. I was also hoping that maybe I could meet my little brother too, though I didn't know if Jeff still lived in that house—or that city.

A woman answered the phone. I asked for LeRoy, and she said he wasn't at home.

"This is Desiree, his daughter."

"I know who you are." She proceeded to rip into me. How dare I call the house, trying to contact any of them, because I have no idea what I put the family through. She said that I bothered them with the phone calls and letters.

I was mad. I told her that all I've ever wanted was to talk to my birth father and find out some information. To try to make some kind of connection. I didn't do anything that had "put them through" anything. Child support was never asked for, each phone call to him never ruffled his feathers. I grew up without even knowing my father and wondering why he never wanted to meet me or know me. I went on to tell her that she had no idea what had been done to ME. Then I took a breath and calmed myself.

"I'm driving through the area. All I want is a minute. To look at my father face-to-face and see what he looks like. I'm told I look like him. I thought I would be respectful to call first rather than just show up."

I had two old photos of him that I had gotten from my mom. I'd once sent LeRoy a letter with a photo of me, including details of what I felt to be features of resemblance to him. He only said that sometimes people just look like someone else. I was left still confused and hurt that he would not say I was his daughter. I also sent letters to Jeff after our conversation, but every time, they got returned to sender.

Anyway, back to the phone call with this condescending woman, married to my birth father, mother of my half-brother.

"It is right that you called first before stopping by. You'd better not."

I hung up.

I was no longer mad. More like sort of numb. I felt that meeting LeRoy was never going to happen. So I quit knocking on a door that would never open.

But I didn't give up on finding Jeff. I thought about him a lot. With the advent of internet and social media, I searched from time to time. In 2011, I was up late one night pouring over social media, trying to find my little brother or wondering if I should give up for good. His full name is extremely common in the Midwest and I did not know where he lived, so I had a hard time singling him out. I decided one last ditch effort to search in a different way. I looked up names I had been given long ago by that investigator. One crumb led to another. Bingo! I found a profile for a Missy with the same last name. She was married to my little brother.

I immediately clicked on Jeff's profile, but it was private. All I saw was a pixel-y photo of a tall 30-something-ish guy and an old guy with a hat and glasses. I knew the older guy was my father. I recognized those eyes. I look a lot like my mother, but I could see my resemblance to my father right away. The other guy had to be Jeff. I proceeded to look at Missy's photos. Boy, was I floored! One of their boys was my doppelgänger! I have never seen anyone in my entire life that looked so much like me!

I decided to send out a message to everyone associated with both of them stating that I thought they could be related to me. This was my chance. To put it out there and know that I did everything I could to contact family, to let them know my side. Unbeknownst to me, Missy had recently gone through something similar with finding family. (What are the odds!) They later told me that when Jeff saw my message, he told Missy he wasn't sure about responding, He'd been told that he didn't have a sister named Desiree, to forget about that long-ago phone call when he was a teen. Missy told him that she was thrilled that she had responded to HER siblings because now her life is filled with more love and joy. She said he should respond because it wasn't my fault, I had only wanted to reach out to find family.

Looking at her profile and posts and pages, seeing so many happenings with my brother and his children, I felt I was getting to know him as an adult. There was a photograph where my brother and father were looking away from the camera. Jeff was standing with one foot forward, arms crossed, like I do. My birth father was standing with the opposite foot forward, his hands behind his back, the way I stand the other half of the time. It was so great to see that because I had never seen that with anyone else while growing up. I hadn't even realized that these two stances were different from the family I had grown up with. It was all starting to click, those other parts of me.

Then I jumped to Christmas of 2009 on Missy's page. I saw a post that said this would be Jeff's first Christmas without his father. I had to re-read it a couple times because I couldn't understand what I was reading. I could not comprehend. I did not want to comprehend. Sure enough, my birth father had died October 2009. I was standing in the kitchen,

Connection, Confession, Redemption

reading on my tablet. My legs got weak. Sliding down to the floor, against the cabinets, I called out for Cindy.

I found his obituary. No mention of a daughter Desiree. Only the two stepdaughters that he helped raise, and his son. It's hard to describe the anger that I felt. The hurt. The fact that even on his deathbed, he couldn't admit that he had another daughter. And that his wife couldn't admit it.

Now I knew that I had lost the chance to ever see my father in person.

A couple days went by before I heard back from Jeff. He said that yes, I have the right person. He told me he remembered talking to me when he was sixteen. He confirmed that he and I were the only children by that father. Jeff and I started messaging back and forth, getting to know each other. We started an online word finder game. It was nice to get to know his brain, too. Very similar. I loved the connection I felt.

Within the year, Cindy and I flew out to meet Jeff and Missy and their family, my niece and nephews! I was so darn nervous, not knowing what to expect. We met up at a nice restaurant. Cindy and I looked over the menu, and I was shocked to see a "Goldschmidt" Winery selection. That was mine and Jeff's great grandfather's name. I was excited now, taking it as a sign that our meeting would be good.

Jeff and Missy walked in, and I could tell that they were nervous too, in a good way. Jeff sat across from me. I felt an instantaneous connection with him. We started finishing each other's sentences right away. It was the strangest thing, the level of comfort. From prior messaging, I knew that they were excited to see my profile, as in the side of my face. I was the only female they'd seen with the same facial features that the guys in the family had. The forehead, the nose, lips.

I looked at Jeff and Missy. With a smile, I asked, "Are you ready?"

They responded right away, yes! We were in a quiet formal restaurant, but when I turned my head, we livened up the place. Showing them my profile with the smile, they both loudly exclaimed, "OHHHHHHH!!!"

It was so fun to see someone else in the same awe as I had when I saw the photo of my brother and father, and when I'd seen my doppelgänger nephew.

The next day I met Jeff and Missy and their kids at a local children's museum. Cindy got a photo of the moment my doppelgänger and I saw each other face to face. It's astounding. All day, he and the other two kept staring at me, with Missy telling them to stop, ha ha. I felt a great comfort, and a belonging that I cannot explain or describe. At one point, the kid in me was playing with these cool lights on a display at the museum. I looked to my left, and my little niece was doing the exact same thing, same hand motions. Very funny.

In their kitchen later that day, me and my big little brother did a sibling-ship DNA test that was requested by someone else in his family. I'd brought it with me. We were laughing, his family and in-laws were laughing, because we stood the same, we walked the same, we acted the same. When the test results came out, we shared more than half the DNA that siblings share. Of course.

I love the fact that a couple years later, I'd be sitting around a campfire with Jeff and his half-sister. We had quite a nice conversation about things in our childhood that we weren't ever told about. All three of us had had questions. I'm so glad that I reached out to find Jeff. Because knowing the how's and why's, and maybe sometimes the other side of the story, can make you feel like a complete person.

Meeting my little brother was remarkable. I share so many of my thoughts, actions, physical attributes with him and his kids. It's like looking into a mirror for the first time in my life, knowing something had been there all of my life, but no place to put it, or to acknowledge it. I am so grateful.

11

I'd like to put in here, to somehow express, how I feel about the siblings I grew up with. I love them dearly, and we also have great connections.

I grew up in a frugal house and that can be tough on everyone. My three brothers slept in one room. Vic, my oldest brother, slept on the bottom bunk of a triple bunk bed that was built by our stepdad. Basically, on the floor. LOL. My sister and I shared a bed for the first sixteen years of my life. Not fun, as I was always worrying that she was going to take all the covers and leave me freezing in the Minnesota cold, in that old 1800's home.

This reminds me of being at work, (I digress!) with the blanket warmers. I have patients that are so thankful for them. Especially when I have my sheets in there, too, so they lay on a warm sheet, and get covered with a warm blanket. They say they wished they had a blanket warmer at home. I say you do! I explain that in the winter, I pull my top blanket off the bed each night, putting it in the dryer while I brush my teeth and wash my face. When I'm ready, I run back down the hall with the warmed blanket and jump into bed. Voila!

Anyway, back to cold Minnesota and my "formative years." We had a wood stove in the basement. We chopped wood year around. My stepdad, Bob, rented a big log splitter that only the boys were allowed to run. I loved it. The sound of the cracking, splintering logs. I loved the smell. And I hated the smell, too. The reason I did not like the smell of fresh split logs was that I knew we then had hours and hours of work. I knew we'd have to stack it all on the log pile. Then clean up all of the wood and splinters from the grass. Later, we'd have to haul wood to the house.

Unlike most kids, I hated summer break from school. I loved being away from home, at school, amongst friends. I much preferred going to school! No chores. We had twelve acres. A big pond that we put in. Over 1500 trees that my brothers had planted for windbreaks. Work on the farm was never ending.

I hated doing yard work. I felt it was tedious and uncalled for. Certain jobs were assigned to me. I had to scythe around the pond. Yes, 10-year-old Desi would be there in the muck, reaching as far as I could, trimming the pond grasses. I'd also have to use a hand clipper to clip grass around the whole house, and all of the trees in the four lawn areas that we'd had around the house.

It was difficult being there on the farm, with the constant work, but also because of having a new father figure at the same time that we moved there. Bob was opinionated and strict. (Um. Hold on. Something odd just happened. As I type this right now, and deleted some unsavory comments about Bob, "his" song just came on the radio. He sang "Before the Next Teardrop Falls" every single time it was played. Bob died in 1994, and I have not thought about—or heard—that song in years. And yet, here it is. Loud and clear on my radio. So.......Hi, Bob. You were the father that raised me, age 5-16. I cannot deny you that role. Thank you.)

Anyway, there are some things that I can say were good about having Bob as a stepdad, as a father figure, in those years of my life. I learned that when something needed to be done, just do it. When I joined the military, and the Drill Sergeant told us to do something, I'd do it without asking questions. Without asking why. The Army had a slogan "An Army of One." What you do affects others. If you fuck up, the whole team can go down with you. When the consensus is do the right thing, the moral majority, we, are better for it. I know that I'd already learned the basis of that from Bob.

I was going to say that I learned to not ask questions, but that's not really it. What I learned was to do the right thing, to have trust in the process. That stuck with me. I still have this as a major guideline in my life. There's always a process. As I reflect back, I see Bob taught me a lot. And I truly am grateful.

As for our cold drafty house, the bedrooms were all on the second floor, and a full open attic on the third. We'd play hide and seek, and although there were many places to hide, I often used the same spots over and over. I'd hide in the wood stove in the summer. Yes, it was cleaned out that well by the boys. And yes, I was that small. And yes again, that's how exacting Bob was with our chores. A damn wood stove was clean enough for a child to hide in/breathe in. I also hid in the hanging snowmobile suits. I'm reminded of that now, when our cat Lilly thinks we don't see her feet from behind the curtains. My siblings must have had a lot of patience with me, knowing I was hiding in the same places, and in full view in one of those suits.

I have an insatiable appetite to learn, and in retrospect, I wish I spent more time with my mom. Learning how to bake and cook. Or learning from my brother Vic how to cook. He was a great cook. Mom is a damn good baker. She made homemade Easter eggs. Chocolate, peanut butter chocolate, white chocolate, butterscotch. She'd make cookies, and have them cooling all over the table. Our black Labrador, Suzie, often reached up and grabbed all of the cookies on the outer edge of the table. We did not have any typical Minnesota Scandinavian traditions, but Mom did make rosettes. She'd take these snowflake shaped iron dipper things, dip them into a sweet batter, and then deep-fry them. They'd carefully be pulled off of the iron, and when cooled, a bit of powdered sugar shaken over them. They were delicate and gorgeous. I'm sure I learned a lot just by being around her, but a more formal teaching session would have been great. Also learning how to sew from her, or how to crochet. She used to make our clothes, and our dolls' clothing. I wish I'd have learned how to play guitar from her, and how to draw, too. Looking back on all of that, she sure is talented!

Mom was a stay-at-home mom when we moved to the farm. Before that, she was a professional country singer. Having us kids stopped that, though, as time went on. Loretta Lynn once told Mom, "If I wasn't Loretta Lynn, I'd swear you were!" After hearing Mom sing Loretta's songs, I agree. She still has a beautiful voice, and it is so lovely to hear her. Hearing her sing warms my heart.

We had a variety of cool animals on the farm. We had two cows, Joey and Lilac. Three buffalo, Tuffy, Muffy, and Buffy. I got to name the baby, as he was born near my birthday. His name was Scruffy. I vividly recall those cold Minnesota mornings. My sister and I took turns going out at five in morning to throw hay over the fence for them. When we were not doing chores, I loved lying there, either on the grass, or on a snowbank, watching them. Seeing their large nostrils snort out air. Watching how powerful they were when they ran. I did a science project on buffalo once. I brought some hair, so the kids could see it and feel it. So soft. And, no, I do not remember the difference between a buffalo and bison. I don't give a shit, really.

We had a crow named Jo-Jo Crow. And later one called Jimmy Crow. They rode on the handlebars of our bikes and ate canned dog food off of our fingers. We also had a raccoon named Bumper, and one named Snoopy. I don't remember which one it was, but one of them bit my foot when I was five or six. I still have the scar on the top of my foot. Vic was holding me, teasing the 'coon with my foot. The raccoon was tethered to a chain, for safety since we were all doing yard work. Mowers, more mowers, a trailer being driven across to the back to pick up logs, etc. The raccoon lunged at my foot, smelling the gum. Whoops. Raccoons make for good chili. Just saying.

I was also run over by the trailer. If you don't have war wounds from living on a farm, you are not either working hard enough, playing hard enough, or not stupid enough to do some of the shit we pulled. Riding our bikes up and over ramps. Once I pretended I was blind, riding my bike down the driveway. I stopped when I hit the barbed wire fence, my hand impaled on the fence. Another time we were riding our bikes down a country highway, down a hill towards a park. I was barefoot, and the tips of my toes were bloody by the time we got to the park. I don't think I told my siblings, I did not want to be a bother. I should have spoken up for myself more.

Back to the raccoons, they were so damn smart. And soft. Cute. And could be mean as hell. I loved to feel their leathery little palms. We'd put peanut butter in the bottom center of a coffee can. They'd go for it. Head first. They'd have half of their bodies inside that can. They were whip smart too. They learned how to open the fridge. Yup. Mom sure was surprised when she'd go get the thawing meat out for dinner. No meat. HAHAHA. The racoons had such soft bellies. I loved scratching their big bellies, but I had to be careful if their sharp teeth or claws came out. We have a largish kitty now that has a similar belly. Soft, but super strong. She reminds me of the raccoons every time she wants me to rub her belly.

We also had a peacock. So beautiful! And guinea hens, chickens, Canada geese, regular geese. The regular geese were named Oscar, Meyer, Weiner, Hansel, and Gretel. One time when it was super windy, our quonset hut's door fell off its rail, landing on Gretel. I was so sad. Poor girl. Next to our farm, Green Giant owned some of the fields. They put fertilizer on them. We think that Oscar ate some of the fertilizer. He died from eating stuff out there. Mom said I held him on my lap when he died. I remember having him in my lap, making sure that since he was so weak, he had someone loving him when he died.

Bob caught an owl once. The owl had attacked our chickens. Bob set up a trap, tethering one of the chickens to a metal post, as bait. So fucking sad and scary, hearing that chicken bite it. Bob shot the owl, but it did not die. He put it in a cage until he figured out what to do with it. For a couple of days, the owl watched us in the garden, turning its head completely around as it followed us as we worked.

I loved seeing the different bugs, and salamanders. I recently saw one of the cool black ones with the yellowish spots on it at my brother's house. I loved it. Reminded me of exploring as a kid. We had a good time exploring everything.

We had five kinds of apple trees. I still love the dark red, crunchy and sweet apples to this day. I was too short to pick apples off the trees, but every day, there were a bunch of apples on the ground. I'd eat so many apples, I'd get the shits. At work now I giggle when giving out apple juice. I call it "crapple juice" or "appoo juice." It makes the kids laugh. Me too. Some trees had huge apples, not tasty though. Mom used them for apple pies and shit tons of apple butter. To this day, I can't stand apple butter. We also had plum trees, and cherry bushes or trees, whatever. Lots to snack on at that farm!

Building forts was also fun. On the ground, and also up in a tree. My second oldest brother was a good builder. He did a great job with the forts and tree house. We also built tunnels in the snowbanks. With the wind blowing all of the snow, we had large drifts. To control them, most people out in the country put up a temporary short wooden fence to guide the snow to settle more where you wanted it to go. We kids loved that. Seriously. Snow drifts so big that we could carve out tunnels and little "living rooms" down in there. Our

Connection, Confession, Redemption

dog Suzie loved to join us too. I loved hiding out as a kid. I'd sit in one of the tunnels, or carve out a bank for myself. I'd eat snowballs until I had to go in, to the bathroom. Little Desiworld. I did not always like how my siblings treated me, so I'd hide. I guess I felt it was better to be alone.

We had a large garden. Stupidly large. I was in charge of beans. There were five rows of beans, each row about 20 feet long. Well, I honestly don't know how many or how long, but it was a lot. I'd be out there, before breakfast on a weekend, picking beans. I felt like it was forever. I'd pull up like every fifth plant by the root. Killing it. Die, you fuckers. I hated them. I hated how my back hurt from bending over. Even more sucky was how my fingers hurt from cutting the ends off of the beans before Mom blanched them for the freezer. I figured less plants, less to pick, less to snip.

We had lots of veggies in that garden. Maybe that's why it was easy for me to be vegetarian later on. Beets, radishes, peas, cucumbers, rhubarb, strawberries. Sometimes corn. Cantaloupe, muskmelons, tomatoes, zucchini. Mom made the BEST zucchini bread. I'd slice it out of the freezer, and put butter on it. She barely baked the top, so it was a little gooey and so so good. We were spoiled by Mom's canning and baking.

We only grew corn part of the time because we got a lot of corn for free. We listened to the CB radio and when one of the kids driving a Green Giant truck announced they needed help in a ditch, we knew there would be a shit ton of corn to be picked up by anyone that got there first. The boys would go get a truckload of corn. We'd spend the next day or whatever prepping the corn for freezing. We had set jobs. Mine was pulling silk off of the ears. I hated it.

That reminds me of when we'd kill a chicken. My job was to pull the feathers off, after it had been dunked in super hot water. Man, my hands would hurt.

So, yeah, life on the farm was not exactly dull. It was hard. But what an experience. Living with Bob was that too, hard but an experience. Bob was a pipe fitter by trade. A Navy man. He was gone many hours, which we were all happy about. He had a prior family, and they had nothing to do with him. He never talked about his past. He did have some photo albums with photos of him around the world, in the Navy. If we asked Bob about it, which we did, he talked about how he traveled, the fish he'd seen, some things he'd done while on travels ashore. I don't remember much of it. Sadly. He didn't share much else. He was so private, I have always wondered why he did not open up more to us.

Maybe he thought we didn't care.

12

That's the thing about me, I do care. Deeply. Shit gets to me and I want to help people. I want to help people with my stories, that's the whole point of me writing. You might not be gay, but you may have been mistreated on some level because you are different. You might not have searched for birth family, but you may feel a longing for connection. You might not have thought about suicide, or lost someone close to you, or anything that I have gone through, but you have felt pain.

You are not alone.

Sometimes we don't think that we are normal, that we're the only ones feeling what we feel. It turns out we have the same thoughts and feelings like more people than we imagined. Yes, we are all unique individuals (and I've been told I'm pretty different!), but we are all human and we all go through shit. And we all can make it through.

I'm a high-energy person. When I wake up, it's rare that I don't have a bunch of stuff planned. My mind goes zero to sixty in an instant. As I get older, I appreciate days where I can go out with a cup of coffee, enjoying the stillness. It's a daily practice for me, calming my mind.

First of all, realizing that I am the boss of my mind and not the other way around is a game changer. For example, when someone says "Monday is a bitch" or "I hate Mondays," they are letting that day rule them. I say let's make Monday MY bitch. I decide and declare that I'm going to have a good day. Monday is a day to do a fresh start. Monday is a kickass kind of day.

But I used to dread Mondays. I had so much anxiety about going into work on Mondays. For years I got nauseous. I don't know why things made me feel this way. For the most part, I know that I feel responsible for so much. Like responsible for making sure each patient's exam went right. Afraid I'd fail. When I was a kid, and I'd do well on my report card or sports, my stepdad Bob only said, "Good," like that's how it should be. Getting on the honor roll, getting to play on a higher squad, it was all expected. I've always put a lot of pressure on myself. It's been some inner work to release the pressure valve.

The first day that I walked into work not feeling nauseous—the first day in my whole career to feel that way—I'd had a few sessions with a shaman. The shaman helped me release blocked areas of myself. To free up, to let go. To properly breathe. When I find myself getting upset or nervous, I have to turn it around in my head, to remind myself that I'm in control. My thoughts and how I respond are up to me.

I had a manager who once told me that she knew how I was feeling without even seeing me yet. She said she could tell by how everyone else was, from the front of the clinic to the back area where I was working. I'm glad she told me because it made me feel more responsible for myself and the ripple effect we have on others. I know I am not responsible for others and have no control over how anyone else thinks or acts or responds, but I can set the tone. I do like to influence others. I like to lift others up. It makes me want to be a better person. It makes me want to put my best foot forward. Because I know that I can be nasty when I'm in a crappy mood. That's something I'm still working on.

If someone makes me mad, I know that I can verbally abuse them in a way that cuts hard. As the youngest of five, and the smallest, I learned to use language rather than physical strength to arm myself or to fight back. I've done it in past relationships. And I know that I can be a real bitch when I think I'm right about something. I may very well be right, but the way that I say it can be cold and callous. When I think I'm right about something, it's like I've got blinders on. Like I said, I can be an outright bitch when I react to some people this way even though I don't mean to.

Like we all are, I'm a work in progress.

I'm trying intentionally to be a better person. I'm trying to spread love. To spread joy. I guess this can be my love letter to the world. My chitchat to the "injured bird people of the world."

Everywhere I go, I like to talk with people. Ask them questions about themselves. Hear their stories. But as people know me will tell you, I love talking about myself. I don't know why. It is what it is. My mother is the same way. But I've learned to ask people stuff about themselves. It's opened me up to such joy.

At work, after I've got all the information about the patient's medical history, I like to ask them silly questions. Like if you had to choose one food that you would eat for the rest of your life what would it be? Or I'll ask them what they had for breakfast. (Most of my patients can have breakfast so it's not a mean thing to ask). I love hearing the varied responses. It puts the person at ease and takes their mind off their medical concerns. I like to make it fun and not so scary, and we start good conversations.

I also like to ask about their plans for the day. I keep it light and I keep them talking. Especially when I am in my scan room giving intravenous (IV) contrast. I keep them talking, adults and kids. Kids often will not tell you right away if they are having issues with the IV contrast. I've learned to watch my patient's breathing. If they start breathing fast, or if they suddenly stop replying to me, I know they are having an issue. Maybe they have an upset stomach, or a sensation that they can't explain. This way I know that I need to ask them how they're doing, in a directed way.

One thing I also love to do is find similarities between people, patterns with them. For example: When I ask the question about one food for the rest of your life, sometimes three days in a row the most common answer is mashed potatoes, or fish, or pizza. I love that. I've also noticed similarities in anatomy. Almost every patient that has six lumbar vertebral bodies versus the usual five also has a short neck. You can't see it with the naked eye, but when I scan somebody's full spine that has this, I noticed a few years ago that I was always cutting back some of the images needed to get all the way through the neck. Yeah, little things grab my curiosity.

Another patten I've found is that the most common population of people who are claustrophobic are people having a knee MRI. I'm not saying the knee thing has anything to with anything, it's just a pattern I have noticed—most people that are claustrophobic happen to be having a knee exam. Or is it the people getting knee exams all happen to be claustrophobic? And the people that are the most jittery are shoulder patients.

Fun stuff.

That's similar to my thoughts on nuclear medicine technologists, art teachers, and laboratory technologists (sorry to my lab tech niece!). The ones that I've met, anyway. I mean this in the best humorous way—I think that they are all off just a little bit, like half a bubble off. (Bob used to say that.) I think each person in those fields is in their own little world. And that is not a bad thing.

Anyway, tangents. I got a million of 'em.

But people are people. And we all have our issues, foibles, phobias, and whatever. When I was younger, I was lost, in so many areas. Now I want to reach out and be that person for someone else who is hurting. I feel it's my responsibility and my duty as a human to do it. So here I am.

As we get older, we realize what is important, most important for us, and for the family that we have developed, the one we have made. There is still an attachment to our old selves, and the family that we grew up in, but the shift HAS to happen that we place value and time to ourselves and our family of choice.

We cannot control how we were raised, but we can control how we live our life going forward. Letting go of blame and resentment and fear can change your life. It doesn't matter what my problems are. I know it's how I look at it; I can help myself overcome.

Connection, Confession, Redemption

In the gay and lesbian world, there are a lot of people who have family members disown them. Unfortunate, but true. The phrase "family of choice" is a common one. Thanksgiving, Christmas, etc., we are with our family of choice. Just like living geographically far from one's family, but this is emotionally far from our families. I have my family of origin , and my family of choice.

You don't have to be gay to know that family ties are often strangling. No family is perfect. I know now that family members don't have to be friends, confidants. You can still let a sibling or family member know that you love them, even if you are not close or have much in common. You can visit from time to time and not have any expectations. Come from an attitude of "I have enough love for our family connection to respect you when we are together. We don't have to agree on things, but we can be friendly."

Being an adult is being firm in who you are, what is important to you. Not letting someone else dictate what you should do, how you should be. No one needs to be an asshole. Everyone can respect each other. We don't owe anybody anything. But we still need to be kind.

And that includes being kind to yourself.

I hope that whatever you may be going through, you can see that you are not the only one. I also hope you know it is time to stick up for yourself. I've learned that I need to live my life for me. When I do, things just seem to work out better. I need to trust in that. When I take care of myself, I can care for others, if needed. Like on an airplane, you put on your own oxygen mask first!

13

I get asked a lot about the military. Why do people join? Sometimes it's automatically expected of you because it's a family legacy type of thing. For a lot of us that grew up on farms, or didn't have a lot of money, the military was a way to pay for schooling. It's also a way, like for me, to get the heck out of where I was.

I didn't feel bad being in the small town I was in; I just knew that the world was a bigger place and I wanted to be out there exploring it. I'd always felt a sense of wonder when I read about different people, cultures,—and food! I also knew that there had to be people out there like me.

Since grade school on, I'd thought about being a teacher, and a 9th grade science teacher is what I'd decided on in 9th grade. I changed my mind in 10th grade, realizing how tough teaching could be, and seeing my teachers take summer jobs and odd jobs to stay afloat. Timely enough, an Army recruiter showed up at school when I was in 10th grade. I decided with the military, I'd go to school to be a laboratory technician. The recruiter said I had to choose something else because there were no openings for laboratory school at that time. I asked for a few other options or something that would be difficult. He mentioned x-ray. So that's how I chose x-ray.

I did have to go to Saint Paul MEPS(Military Entrance Processing Command) station to do a testing to see what areas I'd be good at. I don't know if they still do it now, but back then the military did aptitude testing. They wanted to see what areas we could be useful, where would be a good fit. I scored very high in medical and science.

So I jumped in with both feet to join the military. It sounded fantastic. Yes, I believed all his lies. The recruiter said that even though I was underage, I would be allowed to drink on a military base. You tell that to someone who is 17, and it's about all I needed to hear. He also talked about traveling to all these great places. I was excited to get out there, see the world, and do a lot of drinking while doing it! Ha!

Since I was underage, my mom had to sign the papers with me. I joined the Army Reserves in January 1986. From January to May, I went to Fort Snelling in St. Paul for weekend drills. The formal definition is training in weapons and marching, but the slang use is general training sessions. On weekend drills, we normally worked in our job description. I wore civilian clothes because I hadn't been to basic training yet where uniforms get handed out. At these weekends before basic, I learned about manner of dress, chain of command, and how to do x-rays. Not only was it uncommon for a 17-year-old to shoot x-rays, it was illegal. LOL. But I guess I showed potential and my sergeant there wanted me to get a leg up on x-ray school.

In June 1986 I got on a plane for the very first time and went to Fort McClellan, Alabama. My world view was expanded immediately. It was super hot, super humid, and I did not understand half of what anyone was saying. They thought the same of me. I had a strong Minnesotan accent (think about the movie *Fargo* and you've got my old accent) and I talk fast. One of the drill sergeants made me drop and do push-ups because I talked too fast. No joke! And I almost got into a fight with an African-American girl because I stared at her while she was doing her hair. I'd never seen anything like it before and I was curious. She thought I was being an ass. I had to assure her that I was simply interested because it was unlike what I'd ever seen.

I met some cool people there. We had to buddy up with someone right away and my buddy was a girl from Iowa who was way taller and skinnier than I was. When she had her hat on, or headgear as it's called, she stuck her head forward with her neck out a little, reminding me of a turtle. She went by her middle name, but her first name was Ruby. So her nickname from me became Ruby Turtle.

We had each other's backs. Sometimes we hid out in fox holes and smoked cigarettes. (That's when I started smoking, in basic training.) If anyone of us in our group wanted to do anything off the books, we'd support them in their little adventure. Our wall lockers had a space across the inside at the top that was perfect for hiding small packs of gum. Gum was outlawed. We were marching one morning, and the drill sergeant came up to me, real close. "Soldier! Do I smell JUICY-FRUIT on your breath?!" Gulp and swallow! "NO, Drill Sargent!"

All of us had some kind of contraband. I had a nickname too. I actually had two nicknames. The first I got was from our company commander. Not a good idea to get noticed by the company commander. When you're in the military, you want to be a wallflower. Otherwise they make you do stupid shit. You get volunteered for stuff. They make you paint rocks that line a walkway. Or mow, or do some cleanup duty that sucked. One day while on kitchen duty, also called KP, I noticed a small tear in my boot. I was sad because these boots were getting worn in and comfy. Water got in my boot so I told the sergeant in charge of KP. I got sent to the company commander's office for a tongue lashing. He proceeded to tell me that I was wasting government money. That now because of my boot being torn, I would waste Supply's time by giving me another pair of boots, and I was wasting the Kitchen's time by being compelled to tell the kitchen sergeant all about it. The company commander from then on called me "The Boot Ripper."

The second nickname, "Detent," came from one of my drill sergeants. We were out on the range, practicing with grenades, Claymore mines, and these light antitank weapons called LAWs. When you fire one of these LAWs, you sling it on your shoulder, making sure you aim it down field. To collapse this weapon, you hit the detent button and you could slide it into itself, making it smaller and easier to carry. Unfortunately for me, the fire button and the detent button are very close. Of course the sergeant came by to see what I was doing at the same time I hit the detent button rather than the firing button. Don't make me nervous, man! That's the fun of having 17-year-olds, out there in a mass group, getting to know weapons together.

That fall I went back to complete my senior year of high school. The next June I went down to Fort Sam Houston in

San Antonio for x-ray school. My clinicals (X-ray practice & final testing) were done at Fort Riley, Kansas. When you're in the Reserves, they try to place you for your clinical experience at a place closer to your home of record.

The only neat place I traveled to for the military was Honduras for my first two-week annual training. I had already moved to Kansas by that time, but I was still attached to my old Reserve unit in St. Paul. I met up with our team in Miami. As we flew out the next day to go to Tegucigalpa, Honduras, it was a strange feeling for this rural white girl from Minnesota. There were four of us on the plane that were white. And also only four of us that spoke English.

I had a good time for the two weeks down there doing x-rays on local people. We were set up to help out the Army's Big Red One military base down there. The active duty staff was happy to have us, and they welcomed us into the fold. We got to sit in on some military meetings and briefings. I was impressed and felt special when the Minister of Health of the Honduran military asked a couple of us to take part in one of their meetings. I'm not sure what perspective this 19-year-old had, but I can see now that all input from experiences outside your own is a good thing.

It also made an impression seeing how impoverished everyone was there. Yet they had a brand new soccer field in Tegucigalpa. It pissed me off because it reminded me of how we couldn't afford to get better education in our school, like an expanded library or certain programs, but the football team got anything they wanted with no monetary questions asked.

I went to a local hospital and not only did I see spiders and actual piles of dirt here and there, they had a polio

Connection, Confession, Redemption

ward. 1988, and they had a polio ward there. It made me grateful that I lived in America.

The people we took care of were so nice. There was a couple of siblings that I took x-rays on before their surgery on their feet and ankles for club foot. The little boy's name was Marco. I remember it to this day because he had a little Hershey's chocolate that he gave to me the second time he saw me. He must've been so thankful. And I was thankful for the chocolate, and thankful for his company.

On our arrival at the airport, some liaison told us they would take all of our bags from the airport and deliver them on base. They didn't; they stole our stuff. Because of this, I wore civilian clothes the whole time I was down there. I'm not sure what the locals thought of this kid with flip-flops, T-shirt, and shorts that was supposed to take care of them. Besides that, our radiologist had injured himself and couldn't work while I was there so I had a crash course in doing fluoroscopy and helping to read some of the images that came through the emergency room. Of note about our arrival, the plane flew so low, and so deep into the city, I swear I could see into people's homes, what they were eating for dinner! Man, I was so scared. But thrilled overall for that trip.

At Fort Riley doing my clinicals, I met a woman, we hit it off, and decided that when I graduated I would move back to Kansas and move in with her. (There is a joke in the lesbian world: What does a lesbian bring to a first date? A U-Haul.) Since I was in the Reserves, I could live wherever I wanted to, as long as the local unit offered the job that I did. So in March of 1988, I had my new-to-me vehicle that my brother Vic found for me and I drove away to start the next chapter of my life. I had a nice solo trip down the highway from Minnesota to Kansas, making my own way, my new life yet ahead of me.

I did not like x-ray much. Probably in large part to the limited education and practice the military gave us at that time. The whole x-ray course was six months long. That's one week of NBC (nuclear, biological, and chemical); a couple weeks of general medical orientation; then the teaching of anatomy and x-ray images; and then a few months of clinicals. Clinicals was doing x-rays and practicing. I felt lost and scared while doing x-rays. Now that I think about it, my MRI training was worse, but I was intrigued with MRI, and kept going. I see now that I just was not good at x-ray, which made me not like it. That kind of realization is okay to me now. The older I get, the less I feel that I need to prove anything. I can see now that enjoying something, whether I am good at it or not, is more important to me.

I started working as a prep cook at a bar close to my apartment. It was a lot of fun. I wasn't of age to drink, but the bartender sent shots through the food window for me. The manager got stoned a lot. One time I went back to her apartment over lunch to help her grab some boxes or something. She started to smoke some weed and asked me if I wanted some. I'd only done that one time before in my life, so I said sure. Needless to say, when we got back it was difficult for me to concentrate on anything. It was Taco Tuesday, and damned if I had trouble making the freaking taco. She had to be back there in the kitchen helping me and we were both laughing so hard.

My girlfriend had a close friend, Tuell, that lived on the bottom floor of our apartment. Tuell and I hung out a lot. I got tons of city girl life tips from her. I learned how to play dominoes, how to give somebody "the look" when in traffic, how to properly tell somebody off, and various forms of backtalk. But more importantly, I also learned how to cook greens, and a bunch of stuff within African American culture that I had no idea about. I wish I'd have met her before looking like an ass in basic training.

I later took a night shift seasonal job at the quartermasters on Fort Riley. My friend Robin told me to come hang out with her there on the night shift for extra pay. All we did was use a large steam press to press BDU's ("Battle Dress Uniform"—camouflage tops and bottoms that the Army wore).

My next job was evening and weekend work in Kansas City for an inventory company. The owner picked us kids up and took us to various high end and low end grocery stores. I had a cool calculator that I wore like a bag over the shoulder. It was upside down, but worked great with your left hand hanging by your side. Brilliant. It was wild to see some of the higher end places. The price differences for the same items shocked me.

When I was hanging out with Robin, working at the quartermasters, it left us with a lot of time to do things during the day as we didn't need much sleep back then. We smoked a lot, talked a lot, and played pool. One morning over coffee, she asked me what I wanted for my birthday. I'm kind of an ass, so I said, "Your coffee cup." It was a beautiful handmade cup that an art teacher friend of hers had made in his pottery class. She actually gave me this cup. I still enjoy drinking out of it. I say I'm an ass, because I knew she would give it to me. We're still friends, thirty years later.

Robin did screen printing on the side. It was a neat process and I loved watching her and learning. I still use the screen printing process as an analogy of why MRI imaging takes so long sometimes. Imagine a T-shirt with a screen over it with an image. You take a squeegee with paint, and the more times you squeegee, the better the image looks. Robin also taught me how to drive a standard stick shift in her 1985 Toyota Celica. I know if I were to go back to being that age, I would focus on learning more things like that. Learning as much as I could. And no, I'd never want to go back in age. But I loved that time of life.

And the next job for me would be at the cheese processing plant.

14

Besides work, women, and wine, and learning about all kinds of shit in general, I have tried out a lot of sports, and I love the amount of crap I need to get started. I love having accessory gear, helper stuff. I also love to share things I have learned that make it easier. Like when doing a triathlon, it's helpful to have no tie laces, just pull on and go. And little bikini undies with cycling padding, so you can wear any kind of shorts, and have some cushion while on your bike. Bicycling gloves are a must for me on long rides. There is graduated padding on the glove, at the base of the palm. Keeps your hands angled when on the handlebar, so your nerves from the hand to the wrist are not pressed on. I learned from experience, of course. After one long ride, 100 miles, I could hardly use my fingers, trying to use my limited sign language to chat with a deaf cycling buddy. So I've learned a lot and I love mentoring people.

Since I was a kid, I've had various bicycles. When I was 30, and started riding with my new Austin friends, I had a hybrid bike. It didn't have fat tires like a mountain bike, but the tires were not thin like road bikes either. I liked it, because I could be on the road, and take off into a park easily,

Connection, Confession, Redemption

too. The problem is, hybrid bikes are heavy on the road. And as I learned more about being on road rides with these friends, I realized I wanted a road bike, and why. Your form is different on a road bike, as you want to be more aerodynamic. You have your head down more, your butt back in the saddle, especially on hills. The bike should be lighter, so you are literally not hauling more over all of those miles.

My first road bike was a steel Bianchi men's bike. Back then they did not have smaller frames for women so I got a short bike that was great for my short legs, but it left my arms reaching too far forward, as it was made for a man's longer torso. After doing a three-day ride from Houston to Dallas, my neck hurt a lot, and I had numbness in my fingers. My neck had been strained, the road vibrations taking a toll. I should have known better, as I'd injured my neck in the military a few years back.

I spent a few thousand dollars on my next bike. I'd done very very well with cycling, and in triathlons, but I wanted to do more cycling on its own, not as a multiple sport event. The bike I decided on had some new (back then) technology. Anti-vibration in the posts and top tube (the tube that is from the seat to the handlebars' stem). The bike was carbon fiber, so it was very light, and very strong. My new helmet was better, too. Light and strong, but it also had a lot more ventilation and an aerodynamic shape. I also had upgraded shoes that Cindy had gotten me for a gift. Carbon fiber soles! Shoes are important for distance cycling. As your foot presses against the pedal, you have foot flex. Because of the flex, your foot not only gets tired, but there is a loss of energy and a loss of strength there. Cycling shoes have a stiff sole to allow you to be more efficient.

Speaking of foot flex, I got a cage-type pedal on my hybrid, once I started to cycle more. Rather than just the push action of my foot and leg, my foot could actually push forward into the cage, then down on the pedal, and after your foot came around, you could use your hamstrings by pulling up. I could use more muscles that way. There are "clip-less" pedals, which is a little clip (I know, I just said "clip-less") that the bottom of your shoe clips into. Now, you can push forward, down, pull back, and also pull up. Think about the action of scraping mud off of your shoe, exaggerated. A great cycle of energy! (Did I just make a pun?)

I also purchased a cadence monitor. As you cycle, you should keep a steady cadence, or spin. Makes it easier to go up the hills, for sure. Keeping track of your cadence lets you know even more when you should shift. I see people pushing really hard as they go up the hill, but if they shift and let themselves spin a bit more, there is less torque/pressure on their knees and whatnot. Anyway. I'm not an expert, but there is a shit ton of skill involved in the mechanics of using your energy well. (Using our energy well—what a great metaphor for life!)

You might have gleaned that I get pretty passionate about stuff. Crazy thing is, I loved and hated cycling at the same time. I did love the challenge. As a matter of fact, I researched what I would need to enter the Gay Olympics. (Yeah, such a thing!) I was kicking ass enough that I could work towards this goal, but unfortunately, I had a bicycling accident that although was not bad, it made me shelve any idea of training for anything serious like the Olympics, gay or otherwise.

Connection, Confession, Redemption

A couple years after I'd moved to Texas, I started doing rock climbing. That was so much fun, too! I did not like coming back down, going over the lip of the cliff. As with any sport, there are things you need to buy, rock climbing no exception. Powder/powder bag. Harness that you step your feet into, wear on your pelvis. Lots of carabiners to attach shit to your harness, and carabiners to attach yourself to ropes. Tight shoes, like a size smaller than you'd normally wear. Some people lose or almost lose their toenails because the shoes are so tight. The shoes are intentionally tight so that you can use your toes to get up in those crevices and cracks. I learned how to splay my leg out, my hip, so that the inside of my leg would be flush against the wall. Think about how you should carry a box, against your body, best use of energy. The position of your climbing body is the same, the closer to the wall you can get, the better. Most of the time.

Women's bodies are great for climbing. We have great hip flexibility. I had braces on my lower legs and ankles as a child, since my legs splayed out abnormally. I was born three months premature, so I had some stuff that was just not ready for little Desi to do when I was born. I also was born with cartilage and joint issues all over. I have instability in both shoulders, my jaw is wonky, etc., etc. It's fine, I now know to look for issues, take care of them before I need to. I had surgery on my left shoulder in 2015, five repairs at once. I do physical therapy for my right shoulder. It's all good. Whatever. Just another tale in my overflowing treasure chest of Stories of My Life.

I love sports and being connected to my body. Cycling up a hill gives me a mental focus, similar to the focus that climbing gave me. They are both like playing chess, or like golf. Yes, I play chess, and I learned how to play golf a few years ago. With the climbing, I enjoyed getting my hand and finger grip as strong as I could. Grabbing just a crack in the wall, or a slightly thicker layer on a wall, and pulling myself up gave me such satisfaction. I stopped climbing too because of my neck issues. Looking up while on a wall, or looking up while being the anchor-belay person for the climber, was too difficult and painful. I felt it was not safe for me to look down to rest my head, when I was supposed to be constantly looking up, scanning for issues with the climber. So, yeah, I love sports and being physical. And I can only do what my body allows, at this point. I'm working on more mind over matter.

I was only going to make a passing mention about these physical passions, but my need to share has created more than a few paragraphs here—its own little chapter! It might be more obvious to you now how intense I can get. When something interests me, I am sucked in. I love going all in. It's how I am wired.

I love to learn and I love to teach. It's part of who I am. And loving all parts of me is what I've learned this life is about. And now, hopefully, what I'm teaching you.

15

While I'm in full-on Desi-mode of sharing what excites me, it would be odd for me to not mention another favorite thing of mine....MINI Coopers!

I got my first in 2010. I did not know anything about this British line. Yes, there are other countries involved, but I'm not gonna get into that. My first was a Clubman, "Clubby," two doors, one longer than the other. One side has a suicide door, great for a large opening to put stuff in. There are also barn doors on the back, "Zug" doors. When you buy a MINI, the company MINI USA sends you a neat box, or now a bag, of fun MINI stuff. MINI mousepad, stickers, pen, USB, sunglasses, and the bag actually turns inside out, becoming a backpack. There are grill badges, gloves, shoes, duffle bags in the MINI brand. Cindy and I have MINI fold-up bicycles. So much stuff. And so many individual accessories for your MINI. (They should hire me to be their spokesperson!)

The community is what sold me, and sold my wife, on buying one. Quirky people, out to share, enjoy, motor together. Long roads, twisty roads. I am now on my fifth and sixth MINIs. I bought one last year—on purpose—that needed a shit ton of work. I wanted to know how to work on an engine, body work, vinyl wrap, paint, upholstery electronics, etc. I've done all of that and more. With MINI friends. The latest one is a retired Red Bull vehicle. Red Bull takes the can off the top of it, and sends the vehicle to auction. The cooler is still intact in the back. But the vehicles have high mileage, and need upgrades with maintenance. I'd wanted a little pickup truck, but wanted to stay in the MINI line. So, I've turned this into a truck! I had a truck bed constructed for it. The tailgate had to be repaired, steel bed, liner added, drainage. Before the bed fix, exhaust filled the cabin, as the back of the cabin was not sealed. I had a lot of work ahead of me.

My other MINI is what's called a John Cooper Works edition, a JCW. Special suspension, brakes, seats, added fun. I've only done a couple of things with that one. I've replaced the standard chassis brace with one with less flex. It corners and goes over bumps much smoother now. I also added a carbon fiber cold air intake. Basically, it breathes in better with the intake. The exhaust is already an upgrade, as it is a JCW. The vehicle takes air in and out better than a regular MINI, so it has more power, cools off faster when heated, and the best part is that it has a great burble and pop.

We've traveled 5,000 mile city-to-city charity events with hundreds of other MINIs, friends old and new, put on by MINI USA. Swag, parties, food, all while seeing America. We also like to go to every MINI dealership that we can, all over the world. And get their swag. My favorite was the chocolate shaped MINIs in Belgium. We also bought scarves there, with some symbols that represent the country. It's a blast to see our collected items, knowing where

I got them, and the story behind the travel to get to and from there.

We've gotten mini MINI (no pun intended) fans that attach to your phone, bags, mugs, hats, beanies, and stuffed bulldogs (MINI's mascot due to the car's stance). At a snowmobile museum, we were given ice scrapers with the MINI logo. Living in Texas, we can only use an ice scraper maybe once every couple of years. When our caravan got into Minneapolis, I gave mine to a Minnesotan with a MINI. Another funny item was curly straws, from a straw factory in Ohio. We got cookies in the shape of MINI Coopers from a well-known bakery in Michigan. MINI does great marketing when they roll out a new model or redesign. They gave out MINI Cooper snow globes at one point. I love it all! (Seriously, hook me up with an endorsement.)

Not that you probably care, but a quick note about the spelling/punctuation of MINI vs Mini. Old school is Mini. MINI in all caps is kind of a marketing surge by MINI USA to show a newness to the brand, new style, new consumer base, appealing to ta younger base. I like to use both, it keeps everyone in the loop, involved. It does not matter to me if I write Mini or MINI, I love these cars.

I've learned how to drive a lot better, being in this community of MINI drivers. I had no idea that these were sports cars. A lot of people don't know. I've been on the track with my more powerful MINI, with some great sports tires. I learned from the track owner while he was my passenger, about my driving style, how to corner better, when to gas, etc. The tires I'd researched are fantastic. I have great traction in extreme heat, but also in the rain or colder weather. I absolutely love driving my two

Connection, Confession, Redemption

completely different MINIs. One is a head turner, people are astounded to see a MINI Cooper truck. People of all walks smile so big when they see it! It has a small engine, so we laugh that it's like a lawn mower powering a truck. But it's so light, and has way more power than you'd think. The rear seats have been removed, and of course there is no rear hatch adding weight. Our other MINI is sexy AF. Chili red, British mirror caps, 18" wheels, amazing seats, and a strong burble and pop sound from its engine/exhaust.

So… have I whetted your interest in a new car?! Maybe I like them so much because they are fun, plain and simple. That is how Cindy and I like to live life.

My wife and I laugh, all the time, and have our inside jokes, and truly love hanging out together. We do all kinds of crazy shit. One thing I like to do is play and assume everyone is gay until proven otherwise. I started doing that when I was in Kansas, around a lot of homophobes. It made me giggle each time, which was better than being mad, or insulted, or depressed by the stupid acts of others. I know the ignorant fools were taught to hate, fear, and spite what is different from them. Ugh. So I like to play games in my mind. What if they're gay and they don't know it yet?!

Another head game I play—these are good head games—is when someone across a room or restaurant is laughing, I like to imagine that they are laughing at what I just said. They are my audience and they adore me. There's a quote from the teacher Byron Katie who said, "Everyone loves me. I just don't expect them to realize it yet." Great words to live by.

I wasn't always so sure of myself. Like I said in the beginning, I didn't feel secure in my own skin. I know I am not alone. And maybe my issue of feeling abandoned was simply because my birth dad took off and didn't want anything to do with me. So maybe that's why I never let myself be single, I was always in a relationship. I didn't want to be alone. AND I was always the one doing the leaving. No one could abandon me if I left them first.

Anyway, we all have our shit, and as we grow, it gets better. Life gets easier. I will say it again: You are not alone. Someone else out there feels the way you do.

I watched a show recently, where a girl on the autism spectrum collected business cards. The people around her thought it was strange to have that collection. I looked over at my wife, and told her that I had a nice collection of business cards. My reasoning is that it's a good way to keep track of info, especially nowadays when contacts can get deleted. Cindy raised an eyebrow and replied "and I thought your matchbook collection was weird."

Yes, I have a nice matchbook collection, back from my smoking days. Many of the places are not open anymore, so looking at all the matchbooks is kind of like a journal of places I've been. I've already mentioned how much I love my journals. One of my journals is a keepsake book with taped-on movie tickets, concert tickets, significant fun photos (before social media, when we printed stuff off!). It's still a blast to look at that journal. There is a time stamp, a place, and so many memories attached to those bits of souvenirs. I love my collections.

Watching that show about autism made me think about how I like to think about five things at once, and then figure out how I can get those five things to go together, or be related, or be associated. I can relate to that show, to those kids on the spectrum. I get how things need to be a certain way. How it feels to have blinders on, only thinking of my end goal, of what I know how something should be. If I am about to move a piece of furniture, it's like Tetris, I know how it's supposed to go, how it's supposed to get there. My boss always pulls me to help her load up her wagon when emptying her car with stuff for work. She says she enjoys seeing how I make it fit.

But I admit I get aggravated when those around me don't see things like I do. I've been working on that for a long time. A very long time. I had comprehensive testing a couple of years ago. I did it at first to find out why I have a memory issue. I also wanted to know if I had adult attention deficit hyperactivity disorder. Within the preliminary chat before the actual testing, the doctor commented with a laugh that of course ADHD applied to me. I then did some cognitive testing. I had such a fun time! There were a few tests where I had to mix eye-hand coordination—putting little key-shaped things into a randomly slotted board, and another where I was shown a pattern and I had to put the blocks in the same pattern, time tested for both. The person testing me had her jaw dropped open when I'd finished. I did not know what was going on, so I asked her what was the deal. She said she'd not seen anyone do that so fast, and how did I actually DO that? I explained what I was thinking when I was doing it. I picked up one of the pieces, feeling its shape/angle as I picked it up. From there, I'd scan the peg board thing for the same shape/angle. I guess rather than trying to put the key into the shape I was randomly looking at, I found the shaped hole to match what was already in my hand. She shook her head in awe.

My testing was right hand in the top 99%, left hand (I've lost some dexterity in my left due to prior shoulder surgery) 98%. Neat. It explained a lot. I called my coworkers and apologized for having to have things my way, of not listening to their way of doing things. Knowing now that I saw things differently, I saw the end result, and worked backwards from there. Every one of them said it was no problem, that they'd known that ever since they started working with me. I was surprised and touched. I felt accepted for who I was, and thankful for wonderful coworkers who'd become friends.

I also realized that I've always swapped my numbers. Over and over again. If the number is 2435, I'll put 4235, that kind of thing. But I noticed that if I used only my left hand, I did not make that mistake. Wow.

One reason I want to talk about this here, is to normalize it. To normalize that there are a LOT of us that are just left of center. A lot of people that are somewhere on a spectrum that others will not understand at first, or ever. But that it's okay.

I know some people think that there does not need to be a label for everything. For me, it's helpful knowing that certain attributes that I have, that have made life difficult for me, and/or difficult for those around me, are NORMAL. I like to talk about stuff I've done, I like to be vocal about it, (like talking about being gay in small town Kansas), to help others. So others can see a bit of themselves, or their loved ones, in me.

If that makes someone else feel less alone, and more accepting of themselves, then I feel I am living my purpose.

Let's carry on.

16

When I was in my 30's I did some past life regression stuff. I've always been adventurous, willing to explore all kinds of aspects of life, and how we make sense of it all. As kids, we are never sure what our parents think of us, or at least I didn't know. I wondered: Does Mom have a favorite? Does she love me because she has to take care of me? Or has she always loved me?

That's why I wanted to try past life regression, to get some answers to these kind of questions.

I had a book and a CD, a guide to help you relax and bring forward memories. They've found with doing this type of relaxation, the mind can wander back, pulling memories from our lives, and also from past lives. In my experience from doing it a couple of times, I did not have control of where I went, or how far back I went.

Relaxed, listening to the instructions on the CD, the first thing that came up, the first process in my mind, my first memory, was of me and my sister in the first home we'd lived in, before we moved when I was five. My sister and I are only ten months apart, and we were in highchairs. Seeing both chairs came as a surprise to me, since I did not think we had money back then for two highchairs. Mom was feeding both of us. There was a yellow wall. And that was about all I recalled from that first regression. I asked Mom about it later, and yes, there was a yellow wall, and we had two highchairs. Mom and I had no idea how this regression thing worked, but it was fascinating to "remember" something from when I was so young.

The next thing that came to me while listening to the CD was incredible. I was behind Mom, who was in a hospital bed, but not exactly behind her. Maybe I was in the bed. In the regression, I was trying to get a vantage point to see where I was at, and why I saw Mom laying there, obviously pregnant. I recognized her voice, but I could not see her face. She was in a large bay type area, like in a hospital. There was a curtain, so she was not in a private room. Some guy was there, I could not see his face at all. They were arguing, voices raised. I felt Mom be SO protective of me. There was some finality to what was happening there, with their argument. I felt so much love, so much protectiveness from Mom. I was crying as I came out of that moment in time. Coming back to the present, I realized that I was in the womb.

Up to this time in my life, I'd thought that Mom loved me, of course, but not sure how much she loved me. Like that she tolerated me mostly. I was the last one, a surprise. Growing up, she had a closer relationship with my sister, at least that's how I saw it. When I told her what I experienced in the regression, and that I realized that she really loved me, Mom was shocked, surprised. "Desiree, I've ALWAYS loved you!!"

It was then that I finally knew it. I deeply felt it from her then in that moment as an adult, and ever since I was born. I literally felt her love, so strong, so fierce, so amazing, so wondrous.

Our lives are always about perception. Perception is the key to everything. If I had back then realized that there were things I did not know, or did not need to know, I'd have not felt so bad for myself.

I could have made myself more available to talk with my mom. To not hide out so much. I've already mentioned that Mom said as a kid I would not have said shit if I had a mouthful of it. I can see now that I was in my own way. Usually the person holding me back from anything is me.

How could I look at Mom's relationships with my siblings, and think that it was any better? I did not even try to talk to Mom, or let her know what I needed. I think I made her miss out on some stuff with me, too. I also know that I would have not been so ready to drive away to Kansas when I finished radiology school, so ready to run from family. Sure, when we are young, we all are a little self-centered. We think that no one in our family understands what we are going through. Bullshit. We all go through some kind of angst.

Some of us more than others. So much of the time, we torture ourselves.

I know now, in my 50's, that I am happy to be who I am today. I am also happy that I will not be the same person ten years from now. What people told me about turning 40, and 50, that I would not care as much about "stuff," they were right. It makes me look forward to 60. I know that I will be even more comfortable with who I am, where I've been.

I've also figured out that it's okay to rely on others, that it's not a sign of weakness to trust others. I used to think I had to take on the world alone. I'm so glad that's not the case. I'm so glad I let myself be with Cindy, on every level.

There's a line in a Concrete Blonde song that used to really resonate with me: "The crossroads of a minute, and you and me were in it." In the 90s when the song came out, there were a lot more crossroads for me. And I was in the middle of crossroads with a lot of different people.

Also, when we're young, we think everything seems to hang on a minute. At least I did. I was impatient. I was short sighted. I was selfish. I was an asshole sometimes. I still have some close friends from that time; I am a very lucky person. Those friends knew what I was about back then, and know me now. They knew that I was always trying my best, to put my best foot forward. I still am.

It circles back to perception. That's the hinge that keeps up connected or breaks us apart. When you look back over your life, what stands out? People.

Relationships. No matter who or where, perception is key.

I've tried to work hard to progress in my career, to make my patients feel better, safer, listened to. With my Type A personality, it's sometimes difficult to share thoughts and ideas with my co-workers. I'm high energy and bull-headed. I've also learned that even if I have ideas on exactly how the patient should be taken care of, or when at home I have my own direct plan on a project, I need to take a breath and listen. Even if I disagree, I need to really listen—and to make sure their perception is that I listened carefully, that I took into consideration their plans and ideas. It's opened my eyes up to what I should have been doing all along, because I get more ideas, more thoughts on how to do something. I am not the only one with great ideas!

As much as being young and wild is fun, being older and wiser is awesome. There's a song from the 80s called "I Sing the Body Electric" and there's a line that says "I celebrate the me yet to come." I love that.

I used to re-read a book of poems by Charles Bukowski, putting a bookmark by my favorite ones. It was kind of a way for me to see how much I've changed, or not. To see if I've gained any insights on stuff. I have. And I celebrate the me yet to come.

I've learned to appreciate the me that is right now, the me that used to be, and the me yet to come. It is my hope that you can do the same.

17

I have shitty handwriting. Everyone else in my family has great writing. But I finally don't care. Like the fact that I can't color within the lines. Same thing. Don't care. I think these things bothered others, and so they bothered me. But not anymore. I like not caring so much. It lowers my blood pressure. Makes my face break out less.

Handwriting fascinates me though. I know that mine being different has to do with my family lines. Not knowing anything about one side of my family obviously has affected me, in all kinds of ways. When you don't know your father or paternal grandfather, or when you look like someone that you've never met, you begin to wonder what attributes you have from that person. Even stuff like handwriting.

Handwriting is so personal, so unique to each person. Handwriting is sort of like a fingerprint, an identifier, but one you share with those you love when you sign something for them, like a card or a letter. I love signatures. And I have them all over my body.

It may surprise you, when you see my body, that I'm not a fan of tattoos. It's not stopped me from getting them, but it's stopped me from getting tattoos that do not mean anything.

My first tattoo was with my ex, Kim. I got it early one morning with her. We were sobering up, and a guy with a tattoo trailer was at this monthly German festival somewhere in rural Kansas. It cost me sixteen bucks, all I had on me. Kim let me wear her wife beater t-shirt so the artist could access my skin without me sitting there shirtless. That tattoo was my the first of many tattoos. When Kim died, I knew that any tattoo should mean something. And they do. My tattoos are my life on display.

I got six before I started getting my signature tattoos.

I love my mom's handwriting. I love her signature. I'm sentimental, so I've saved a shit ton of cards, letters, and notes from friends and loved ones. I decided I wanted to get a tattoo of my mom's signature. I also wanted a tattoo of my maternal grandmother, Lorraine. I know that she is always around me and I wanted a picture of her, as a tattoo. Problem is, there are too many crappy tattoo artists, and the good ones are crazy expensive.

You know how things happen in three's, right? And they should be taken note of? Well. Austin has many tattoo parlors. When I decided I wanted a tattoo, bam, within one week, three different people I know posted on social media about this one tattoo place. So I knew that was the place for me. I went online to check out the artists and their work. I saw a large tattoo of Marilyn Monroe, with her signature. Very well done. I sent that artist an email, asking about what I wanted done—a signature, and perhaps a photo. He emailed back right away with great pricing and an appointment time within a week. I was ecstatic, for the doable cost and having it done so soon.

I called Mom and asked her to send me a few samples of her first and middle name, as I did not have her middle name on any letters or cards. As I waited on her, I sent the tattoo guy a photo of Grandma on her wedding day. She looked so beautiful. She was a rabble-rouser, so the pic did not really fit her character, but I still loved that photo of her. It was the one I'd wanted tattooed for a while.

I didn't get Mom's signatures for a few days. By the time I did, I was so excited by my artist's commentary and pricing on my grandma's photo. I decided to go ahead with Grandma's pic. I feel her around me all the time and I've had many experiences, besides angel readings and such, where I knew for certain she is always with me. People get hits that Lorraine with the bright red lipstick is with me, and I just know it. She is.

Deciding to get her photo as my tattoo, I calmed my mind, closed my eyes, and asked Grandma what I should have tattooed around it, to bring it all together. She responded like, duh, SIGNATURE. That funny woman. Of course. I dug out a "Love, Grandma" signature that was on the one birthday card I'd had for forty years. I sent the signature over to my tattoo guy.

When I arrived for my appointment, I brought a few more pictures of Grandma, so he could get the real essence of her. Like I said, the proper wedding picture was not really how she was. He looked at a couple photos and said, "Man, she was a real pistol!"

I flinched, in a good way. "Where did you get that word pistol from?"

He shrugged. "I don't know. It just came to me."

The prior week, I'd gone to a guy who talked with the dead, trying to find out information about my mom's father. Grandma Lorraine told the guy, "That Desiree, she sure is a pistol!"

Connection, Confession, Redemption

Yeah, Grandma and I are connected.

I chatted with the artist, and he asked how I found him.

"Three times in one week this parlor was on my social media feed. So on Tuesday, I checked it out. And emailed you."

"Tuesday!" his face lit up. "That was the first day my work was put on the website. I only moved her two weeks ago. Nice timing!"

Coincidence? Hell, no.

The tattoo and signature turned out beautifully accurate. I posted pics on my social media. One of my uncles was like "Hi MOM!!!" I got a lot of holy shit type comments, a lot also commenting on how much I looked like my grandmother, which I loved.

This commenting went on for a while, and being a Sunday night, I had to get to bed. It was late. I decided to look at one more post—which clued me in that it was Grandparent's Day!

Holy shit. Well played, Grandma. Happy Grandparent's Day indeed!

18

Everyone has an opinion on tattoos. I already told you I'm not a fan. Especially of sleeves. I also don't think people should get them when young. Or drunk. And I've done all those things. Both arms are now covered. I get surprised in pics sometimes, like, wow, that's me!

Yes, I was young when I got the typical rose on the boob. I laughed, figured it would be a long stem rose when I got older. Now I know that shit ain't funny. (Well, yes it is.) Twenty years later, I got it redone. I had the colors brightened up, and added a few more leaves, extended the stem a bit.

In the 1990s, it was common to see sun and moon drawings for various stuff. I've mentioned my love for the band, Concrete Blonde. The first time I heard a song of theirs and saw them on MTV, I was smitten. I've seen them or versions of them/their lead singer twenty-six times since 1990. Safe to say, I love them. They used a sun/moon combo on one of their album covers. I had that small drawing used as a tattoo on the back of my right shoulder. I got that redone years later, too. Brightened it up, and added about ten inches of artwork from another Concrete Blonde album cover.

Connection, Confession, Redemption

Another tattoo is on my foot. I love walking on the beach on vacation and taking a picture of my feet in the sand. I decided I wanted a smiley face on the top of my foot. When I moved to Austin, I noticed that whenever anyone got in an elevator, they looked down. No one smiled. So I wanted a smiley face smack dab in the middle of my sandal. My brother, Vic, was with me when I got this tattoo, which was painful. As I tried not to cry, Vic sat by me, taunting me with a laugh and a "Don't be a pussy!" That day has become a great memory for me. Interesting to have a guy who helped raise me watch me get a tattoo.

I now take my "my foot is in" photos, and make sure the smiley face is in the pic. Yup, I've taken pictures around the world of my foot. When I see a manhole cover that has the city name on it, I love it. Sometimes they have a local symbol on their manhole covers, like in Philly with the Liberty Bell. Better than a postcard for me. I used to buy postcards to save in my journals. They have good photos of the area, good information on that place or city. Manhole covers with my smiley faced foot are some of my fave photos.

A year after I started dating my future wife, we were in the middle of nowhere East Texas. Cindy's cousins were getting tattoos, and I decided to get one, too. The tattoo place did not impress me much, but I wanted to do something with the cousins. I got a small tattoo—Cindy's name on my right ring finger. I was SUPER nervous about it, as it was quite a statement when at work. You know, the gay thing. But I wanted to move forward, and yet again be like everyone else. Get what I wanted when I wanted.

Back at work the next week, I never said anything to anyone. When a patient asked what it was (you could tell it was fresh), I said "Oh, it's a name," if I felt they would be judgy or a homophobe. I've learned since then, that I don't always need to "be me," that it's okay. I still sometimes tell someone it's a name, rather than tell them it's my wife's name, if I think they are going to act differently towards me. Some people are not worth the effort.

In between the addition to the sun/moon tattoo, I got another big tattoo. As you know, I am a Minnesotan. Too many people think that it's just cold there, all the time. It's not. It's beautiful, with summer green grasses, blue lakes, with red and golden leaves when it turns Fall. I added a pretty reddish-orange Canadian maple leaf. To the right of the Minnesota tattoo. As a nod to my Canadian neighbors to the north. When I started doing my ancestry a couple years later, I found out that I was also Canadian. Very nice.

I started getting interested in DNA when I turned 40. Before that, I'd had a passing interest, but without having a paternal DNA connection, I could not move forward with my ancestry. The National Geographic Genome Project's DNA test kit was a gift from Cindy. I was appreciative of the thought, but she did not realize that I needed paternal DNA to figure out anything about my ancestry, so I was still at square one. Cindy told me to read the kit's pamphlet. Stubborn, but curious, I opened it. It said that only my DNA sample was needed. I was excited, knowing that this was an actual start!

As I thanked her for finding this for me, I looked closer, seeing MY actual kit number! I was overwhelmed. I was overjoyed. I could not comprehend what was in my hands.

Cindy grinned at my confusion. I asked how she got this sent in. She explained that when she'd asked me to spit into a test tube to test for the swine flu, it really was for this DNA sample. Sneaky woman! I love her!

I typed the kit number into the web page. Up came my actual DNA history. WOW. For the first time, I felt like I was someone that came from somewhere identifiable. I felt grounded, and also that my life had no limits.

In about 2012, I started doing more research. I wanted to find more information about my birth father's side of the family and my mom's birth father. As I discovered more people, I was intrigued to see my lineage, to see the tree unfold and grow. Last names started to mean something to me. I began collecting any signatures that I could of direct ancestors. A signature is such a calling card for me. I'm sure that in the past people made a point to not scribble their name. I admire some of the gorgeous penmanship that I have seen and gathered. I don't have too many photographs of my ancestors, which makes their signatures even more special.

I talked to my tattoo guy about adding signatures to the ones I'd already had—Mom's and Grandma's. He suggested putting them on yearbook style, which is not lined up at all. That way I could add on as I wanted and no name had to be coordinated with another one. I liked it. I decided to keep all the signatures on my left arm. As I found more family, and I verified that this was indeed the person of my ancestry, I had them added on. I've only added one family branch, one family name from each line. I will not use a signature of a female signing their married name. That's not her ancestral name. I am finding out who I am, where I came from. It's important to me to represent this correctly.

Finding a signature is not as easy as you'd think. To this day, I still can't find my birth father's signature. I found his father's from a military draft card. Common places to find signatures are on wills, draft cards, property transfers, and letters to family. These kinds of things used to be more of a public record, but with identity theft, it became much harder to find someone's signature. Verifying is pretty easy when there is other information on the document that matches specifically to that person. Date of birth, address, associated person, those types of things. All of these signatures, along with Grandma's portrait, are on my left side.

My piles of cards and letters from various people over the years had been unwittingly kept for a new reason, signatures. When a sibling or relative wrote a nice salutation, I definitely kept that card or letter. I like these mementos for keeping track of stuff, like a diary. I think I also kept them because it logs the fact that I was thought of. That I meant something to someone. Enough that they wrote to me, for whatever reason. Nowadays, people text, or email, but there is rarely a handwritten word, or signature. So I keep them.

A couple of years went by before I started to think about what I'd like to have on my right arm. I thought about a monkey (more on that later). It hit me, as we were driving back from Cindy's high school reunion. I felt that I was now a part of her whole life, as I got to visit with people that had known her for so long. I had kept a fax that she'd sent me ten years prior, for testing purposes to make sure my home fax worked. Yes, we used to have not only work faxes, but home faxes, too. The fax said, "I love you Sweet Pea, Love Cindy." I had kept this paper with me for many years, in whatever bag I was using. It meant a lot to me. I decided to have my right arm be my "love" arm: signatures and salutations of love. With her ok to do it, I got that line put on my right arm. I love it!

A couple of years later, my god son/nephew Cole died suddenly. I'd had cards from him, of course. I put "Love, Cole" on my right wrist. I can see it all the time, just like I can see my mom's signature on my left wrist. At the same time, I added salutations from two of my brothers, as I had theirs ready. One was of my brother Victor. Vic, the oldest sibling, was like a father to me, but also one of my best friends. I love that I can see Vic at any time I want, wherever I go. I'm so glad that I got his loving words put on my arm forever.

I have people stop me on the street or in a store and ask what these tattoos mean, who are these people. I can tell that their heart is so open when they are asking. Sometimes it's fabulous being an empath, feeling that kind of love.

That's why I do it, why I have these tattoos. They are love, on display, and emanating out into the world.

19

When my brother Vic passed, I did not understand exactly what I was feeling. I had a sadness, a disconnect. A hole in my life, in my heart, in my exact BEING. The loss of a sibling is not talked about as much as other deaths. The death of a parent, the death of a child, the death of a spouse. The loss of a sibling is not appreciated, yet is its own incredibly painful experience.

That sibling might have been the first one to see you walk. The one who taught you how to tie your shoes. That sibling might have been the one you talked to about Mom, or other siblings, or life. They were your confidant. Your mechanic. Your go-to person for that family recipe. My brother Vic was exactly these things and more. For 51 years, he was that. Things I might never tell anyone else, I could tell Vic.

Before one of Vic's many surgeries, he was feeling down, not surprisingly. My sister and I took him to pre-op. We were in the elevator, trying to find something to make him laugh. Man, Vic had the best laugh. His head would throw back as his whole body erupted with laughter, and you'd hear so much joy!

Connection, Confession, Redemption

We wanted to encourage him. I looked at him and simply said, "Hector, you got this."

My sister looked at both of us, not understanding. "Who is "Hector?" she asked.

We explained that I called him that. She was surprised.

"For over 40 years, you've called him that, and I had no idea!"

Vic laughed, and said, "Yeah, and I call her Residue."

We all laughed so hard. It was a fun moment as siblings. Just when you think you know someone, it's wonderful to find fun private things about each other, things that we share with each other.

The loss of one of "your own" is the loss of that connection, that part of yourself that is now gone forever. That person cannot be replaced. We other four kids talked about this, the hierarchy that had changed when Vic died. Who is our leader? Who do we go to for all of these things that he did? Each of us viewed him as our go-to person. I never knew that. Siblings are not supposed to have a favorite. We do, but are not supposed to talk about it. Now we knew. Vic was all our favorite. We decided that no one could take his place. That no one needed to. We let Vic take that honor with him.

My siblings have taught me so many things, like how to tie my shoes, how to throw a football, how to cut firewood. They've influenced my music selection, even to this day. When a sibling is gone, when that connection is cut from your life, it's hard to deal with. There are stories, conversations that I've had with Vic that I've had with no one else. He always listened non-judgmentally. He was also our buffer for the family. He knew how to talk to each one of us, to relay information if needed. As the oldest, he saw all of us grow up. There is a huge hole where my brother was. It can't be filled. All I can do is accept that reality.

Near the end of his life, I was able to spend a lot of time with him. The best time with him in a long time. He was chatty. Coherent. We watched a boxing match and TV together for about three hours. Ok, it was exactly three hours. I remember it was so fantastic that he was doing so well. And I cherished every moment with him.

I left, as usual not knowing if I'd ever see him again. I took note of the staff that was around him, the walls, the colors, as much as I could fit into my brain. I guess so that when I was on the phone with him or family, I could envision his surroundings. Maybe his last surroundings.

The next weekend Cindy and I were in Florida, visiting with a couple of her sisters. I knew that Victor was going to go soon. I felt it. Then Mom called, telling me that if I was going to come, I'd better get on a plane now.

I had the knowing that it would not have mattered, I probably would not get there in time. My other siblings firmly told me it was okay to stay in Florida. They wanted me to be with Cindy and her family. They said my previous weekend with Vic was the best time that I'd had with him in a long time. I let that be my memory.

Cindy and I and her family were at a beach restaurant, finishing lunch. I KNEW I had to get down to the beach, to get a photo of my smiley face tattooed foot. The Sarasota sand is very light, and can be blinding in the sun. I tried to get a decent photo, but with that phone and the glare, I could hardly see my foot in the viewfinder. Finally, I got a good shot of my foot and my tattoo.

Then a text message came in from my family. All caps. My brother's name, his date of birth, and date and time of death.

I dropped to my knees, crying. With the waves crashing on me, I looked at my phone. There it was. The exact time I got the good pic of my foot, the tattoo I'd gotten with Victor, was the exact moment of his death. I was so full of love, and joy, and anguish, all at the same time. I knew it was okay that I'd stayed in Florida when he was leaving. I am grateful for the message I received. I knew Victor was just fine. I felt so thankful. He was with his son, with family, and God.

And I know that Victor is with me. Like I know that my Grandma is with me. And I also know that God is with me. I am not alone. I have a safety net because of that. Things will ultimately be all right. I have that connection myself now too, and it makes all the difference.

Desiree B.

20

I'm excited to add a couple more signatures on my left arm. One is of my 8th grandfather. He actually has a few hundred descendants and a nice place in American history. There's an academic hall named after him in Ohio. It's all pretty cool. I'm also going to add on a 9th grandmother. She could not write. On the signature line, someone else wrote her name, and she put an X underneath it.

Finding all of these names was not easy, but it's something I love to do. I love the journey. I love hearing about American history because now it pertains to me. When I read about it now, I can retain it. Reading about the history of when my ancestors left different countries is interesting, too. I now know that my ancestors left Cornwall because mining there within the dates they'd left was not fruitful. They left for America to continue mining. It has also been fun to research a certain year when someone came over to see what else was going on in the world. What inventions were coming out, what health crisis was going on at that time. It helps me with context.

On an early drive back from Dallas one morning, trying to stay awake, I was searching for channels on the

Connection, Confession, Redemption

radio. On a local NPR station, I heard a distinctly British type voice, but it was clearly an old recording. I could not place where in Britain the accent was from. Turns out, it was an interview with a Cornish miner. I loved it! That was exactly how my ancestors sounded. I've read that Cornish people don't consider themselves British, but just Cornish.

My grandfather Goldschmidt was a miller. He arrived in Minneapolis from Hungary at about the same time as William de la Barre, the man who opened the Washburn Mill in 1880. At the time, it was the largest flour mill in the world. The Washburn Mill would join to make General Mills. One nickname for Minneapolis is "Mill City." It's pretty great that my third grandfather took part in that. I remember when I read about where he worked. Cindy and I had visited the Mill City Museum a few years before. It had been the mill he worked in! I cried, I was so touched. I had stood in the same room that a grandparent had been in. I have no idea what he looked like, but I'd been where he'd been, and I have his signature.

I have his signature on my arm, and also have his wife's, Minnie Ernberg. She came over with her family from Sweden. Her family settled part of southern Minnesota. I thought as a child that I didn't have any ancestry or history. I was wrong. I made a point to travel to visit the gravestones of her and her siblings, in southern Minnesota. It brought me so much joy to see all of them lined up. For me, seeing my great grandmother's gravestone was the next best thing to meeting her at a family reunion.

One thing that I've enjoyed about my research is the similarities that either I'd known about or discovered by seeing a whole family line. Like how many religious scholars, preachers, and founders that we have. In quite a few different religions. At one point, I have two 11th grandfathers that HAD to have been in the same church. One was Quaker, and one was Church of England. There was a discussion of course about the takeover of the area in Pennsylvania by the Quakers. Being two prominent religious leaders, my grandfathers were there together representing their opposing communities. It's neat to think about how hundreds of years later, they're connected again, by my family.

The physical similarities have been great to see too. The women in our line have small heads—pea heads. LOL. I always wondered where they were from. We also have high cheekbones. I saw a photo of Mom's 3rd grandmother. Wow. Same hairline, same way she stands, same way her hand is placed on the person sitting in front of her. And of course, same pea head and cheekbones. Even Mom was floored to see the uncanny resemblance. There's also a 3rd grandfather of hers that had nice wavy, dark hair. Same part in the hair, same wave that Mom has. A very prominent wave. I love it.

I know I'm on the right trail when researching when I see a name being used throughout the family. Like our Teetzel line has a lot of Williams. And a few Jonathans, with no "H." There was a Marlon Teetzel up in Canada. I saw a great great nephew of his, down in Michigan. Middle name was Marlon, so I knew the nephew connection was correct. Things like that. I love connecting the dots. My great grandmother's name was Elsie. When researching cousins in Minneapolis, I saw an Elsie Teetzel. I knew for sure that she had to be a close relative, and I was right.

Connection, Confession, Redemption

When I told my Mom that I think I found a close relative of hers, Mom gushed about how she actually remembered Cousin Elsie. Lovely.

I love to find and contact cousins. Finding relatives, discovering information, researching family brings me so much joy. I also enjoy helping others find family.

A Swedish cousin from Seattle contacted me a few years ago. He was not sure how to reach out, since he was adopted, but our DNA was a match. Fast forward only a few months, and I helped him locate and connect with half-siblings and cousins. He has eleven half-siblings. It was awesome to see his family unfold and for him to make beautiful bonds.

Finding family, seeing attributes in others that I've never seen before is a great journey in itself. I love seeing my brother make a face or a gesture that I know I've made a thousand times. It's comforting. Silly traits, like how my upper lip sweats, is the same as my little brother, Jeff. Same gap in my teeth. My high forehead, gums showing when I smile, my nose. I knew that I had physical features that differed from the siblings I'd grown up with, but wow, it was another thing to actually see these on someone else.

One of Jeff's sons told me that I reminded him so much of his grandpa, my birth father. Not meeting the man, it was nice to hear about a connection, that more of me "came from somewhere." I asked my nephew what exactly was similar. He said he could not put his finger on it, but I was just "so much like Grandpa." The way I stood, held my cup of coffee, my demeanor. It felt nice to know that.

I suppose a lot of how we process life boils down to perception. I have plenty of traits from my mom that I love, and there are many things that I share with the siblings that I grew up with. I also know when it comes to nature and nuture, I gained insight and attitudes that have served me well because of my stepdad, Bob. He might not have been "nurturing," but you know what I mean.

I am who I am because of all of it. My mom didn't know much about her own birth father, but it never tormented her. I always was curious. I wanted to know about the other half of me. Now I do. Now I feel whole. But the truth is, I always was.

21

On my Mom's side, there are a lot of us that have "abilities." When Grandma's husband died, she knew about it before she was told. Grandma would call our farm to ask about one of us, specifically. Mom would confirm that that child was sick or got hurt that day at school or whatever. Grandma already knew it. Stuff like that. Happened frequently. Was normal. But never really talked about. For sure Mom and I know when the other is calling. Or if something is up. There are others in the family that also feel this unspoken connection. Mom's brother knew when his father passed. He was out of town with friends. He woke his buddy up, telling him that he needed a ride back to Minneapolis, immediately. He did not tell his friend why. He just knew that it was his dad. We have what some call a "knowing."

When I first talked to one of Mom's cousins that I'd found on an ancestry site, I outright asked her what abilities she had. She said oh, I talk to people all the time that have passed on. She said yeah, there's just stuff that I know. We laughed about that.

So. Fast forward a bit. This cousin, Nancye, had cancer that came back. She posted on social media that she needed prayers and was starting chemotherapy again. At that moment, I was trying to get rid of a migraine. I focused on Nancye, so I could send her my best vibes. I had to focus hard, because of the migraine. Suddenly I felt overwhelmingly in pain, all over. And I felt so nauseated, I practically jumped to the sink, ready to vomit. I started crying hard, and loudly. Vic had passed a few months before, and Cindy, per my request, stopped asking if I was okay when I was crying so damn hard. Well, my crying was so loud, and I guess so different, that Cindy came to check on me. I told her I was feeling what Nancye was feeling.

I called Nancye and she confirmed it was exactly how she felt. She also told me she knew of a fabulous woman in Minneapolis who does this for a living, an empath who takes this pain away from cancer patients. Nancye said I should do that. I had that ability.

I knew I could do it. But again, fear stopped me. Fear of success, fear of people not believing. Plus, why the F would I take on someone else's pain? It's horrific.

Sometimes, as an empath, it's helpful for me to share with someone the physical feelings I get from them. They know they are not alone, that I literally understand what they are going through. Because I feel it.

I also clear bad shit, bad energy, too. My first experience when I came out of the closet for doing this kind of work was with a coworker and lovely friend. She come in to work one day, and her energy was so heavy, so sad, so painful. I see colors and she had brown all around her, and a bad bad feeling. She was about fifteen feet away from me when I told her to not come any closer. I couldn't take it. I wanted to cry, it was so bad. I reached out, and with my mind and my hands pushed away the energy that was surrounding her, from my distance. It helped, so I could be around her. She said she felt lighter immediately. A couple of hours later I was able to spend some time with her. I worked to push away, to clear her funky energy. She was overwhelmed with gratitude. It gives me great pleasure to be able to help like that.

I told my friend Margaret about this incident, and she asked me to do the same thing for her, to help assist with what was going on with her. She knew that I was an animal communicator and she knew I had helped over a hundred people with their pets. Margaret knew I could help her. I calmed my brain, thanked God for the ability to open and communicate. I told Margaret what I found, and it was spot on. I was able to clear her energy and help her heal.

Back in Kansas when I had started to learn color therapy, it was simply because I saw a book on it, and it interested me. I used cue cards, for practice. I had colored a few, and on the back wrote down what each color was for: blue for cooling, red for warmth, white and silver for healing, green for growth, yellow for moving stuff along. That type of thing. I'd close my eyes, shuffle the cards. I'd place my hand over one of the cards, feel what vibrations came from the card. I got pretty damn good at it. The easiest colors for me to apply are white, blue, silver, and green. Maybe because they are more general, more healing type.

If you have never worked with energy, put your hands almost together. You can imagine a connection there. A feeling, a force pulling them together. Imagine that. See if you can feel a pulsing. When you imagine the energy, it helps you to actually feel it. That's the energy that is used

Connection, Confession, Redemption

to push or move someone else's energy in their body. I do it while also imagining the vibration of a certain color, depending on what I need. For example, green and yellow has been helpful for clearing sinus issues.

Today I am not so shy about my abilities. I know I can help people, and if I can help people, why in the world would I not? I now do remote and in-person energy clearings and communication. Knowing how I can do it with animals, people were the obvious next step.

My brother Jeff is a busy guy so we don't chat all that much, even though we are very connected. I could feel he had issues he was not telling me. I messaged to ask if he was okay. He replied back: What do you know?

I quieted my mind and concentrated on him. I told him what I felt from him. Low back pain, more into left leg, with the left foot forward making it worse. He was like WTF mind blown! Jeff had exactly what I described. He asked how I knew, and I explained that I focus and let the person's body communicate with me.

He's now a believer. Not everyone is. And that's okay. I am slowly getting over the fear of others' opinions. If they believe, great. If not, maybe eventually they will. I know I need to continue. I need to help others heal, and heal myself when needed.

When I set out to write this book, I thought it was going to be something different, just a telling of my funny stories. But it seems like self-acceptance is the message needing to come out. For me. For you. For all of us.

In my memory, I see myself as scared a lot as a kid. I've reconnected via social media with a former elementary school teacher of mine and I asked her about my demeanor during that period. She said all that she can remember is that I was a bright, bubbly little girl. That the room would shine when I was in it. She said I was a champion of rights, standing up for others, outright saying "That is not right!" and arguing my view, or the other person's cause. She recalled how I would also tell someone that that's not the way to be, the way to act towards someone else. She said that I did it in a great way, because my classmates took it very well.

Isn't that funny, how I could see myself so differently? I know that I became angry later in life when things weren't fair. And now I know it is not bad to be angry. How we deal with our anger is the key. I can be angry about how gay people are treated and that anger launches me to speak up. I see how I have helped various coworkers be more understanding about how gay people are REGULAR PEOPLE! I guess I do more good than I realize. I think we all do. We tend to fall back into old patterns of seeing the not so great things about ourselves, instead of seeing how much we have grown.

Sure, I've had temper tantrums and plenty of behavior that I'm not proud of. And I have plenty that I have done right, that I am proud of. Yeah, I'm full of stories and bullshit, for sure, and I'm also full of compassion and empathy. There's been a shit ton of woo woo stuff in my life, and I no longer need to hide it. It's part of who I am.

And I now, finally, maybe, accept all parts of me.

22

A couple of years ago, a close friend asked Cindy and me if we wanted to smoke toad. Like for real, a South American toad that is dried and you smoke it. Kind of like the plant medicine, Ayahuasca. You do not control what comes out; what comes out just does. It's sort of like a spiritual journey, to get more insight into yourself. We said sure.

So. Backstory. I love monkeys. I have felt the connection of being monkey-like. I love the playful nature of monkeys. I have collected stuffed monkeys for my workspace. My MRI scanner is decorated like a jungle, lots of monkeys. I have felt somewhat odd, being of this age, and feeling like a kid, like a monkey. But it is what it is.

Cindy and I went to Dallas, to smoke toad. The lady that was the practitioner, the guide, if you will, had rented an apartment above our friends' place for the weekend. Other friends had come for sessions too. Cindy and I decided we only wanted one.

In the upstairs apartment, the practitioner and I sat on a blanket, near the French doors near the balcony. In her mellow calming voice, she said, "I will be here the whole time with you. You might feel things, and experience things, and go places perhaps. But you will physically remain right here, on this blanket. I will be here with you."

I said, "Let's do this," and took a toke of the toad. Too bad we didn't video the experience.

I remember knowing stuff. Like, just knowing. Experiencing things on a depth and level that I now have no comprehension of. I knew that my grandfather Goldschmidt (the miller from Hungary) is with me, guiding me financially. I knew my grandmother was with me, guiding me in all kinds of ways.

But I remember also being so scared of the feeling of vulnerability. So scared, that I had a hard time breathing. I thought I would die. I was afraid of death while under the influence of toad. I also had the feeling of stuff coming up out of my throat. The practitioner said that was common when someone was trying to speak up, get their voice heard. I went back and forth from being "in toad" and conscious. I remember feeling a lot of saliva. Like drooling saliva, wiping off my tongue on anything available.

Then I felt like I was a Buddha monkey, sitting there, cross legged. (I was physically laying down the whole time). I laughed and laughed. Floating and laughing. Laughing SO MUCH. Giggling. So happy. So free. Laughing when I realized that I AM A MONKEY. I realized that it was OK TO BE A MONKEY. That brought me so much joy. The knowledge that being a monkey, of a monkey, the essence, took over all fear of death. It took over any other confusion or fear that I had. I felt SO GOOD. I was at peace with myself.

When I was fully conscious, or rather, able to leave the apartment, I started to put my shoes on. I only got one on, because I did not want to put them on. I wanted to be free and playful. I saw a bowl of fruit, saw bananas. I grabbed a banana. I showed up in our friend's apartment, giggling still. A shoe in one hand, and a banana in another, saying "I'm a monkey, I am REALLY a monkey!!" My friends said in unison, "WE KNOW!!"

I learned that it is okay to be a monkey. It's okay to be who you are. It's okay for me to be silly. It's okay for me to be who I am. Because I know that I am damn good as a monkey.

I know my purpose here on earth is to spread joy. Over and over, and over. Spread joy. If that means being playful like a monkey, so be it. Monkeys are smart. Adaptive. Fast learners. Curious. Always busy. Clever. Creative. Need stimulation.

For sure, I am a monkey.

And yes, I now have a tattoo of a monkey.

23

You know the importance I place on ancestry and names. It's interesting, then, to see that I have taken my wife's last name as my own.

Doing my ancestry and genealogy, I did not like the fact that women had to take a man's name when they got married. I loved the reasoning behind the Latino population's keeping the woman's maiden name, along with her new last name. She is honoring both branches of her family tree.

I began to see this new family name as a whole new branch for the ancestor taking on a different last name. She was not genetically related, but this was in fact her new family. Whether she was going to have children or not.

In 2015, Cindy and I were going to celebrate our 10-year anniversary of being together by taking a two-week trip. I asked her where she wanted to go and what she wanted to do. One year we went to Vancouver, Canada. It was fantastic, as the weather was beautiful, plus when Canadians celebrated Canada Day, we pretended the fireworks were for us.

Cindy did not have any ideas, so I said, "Let's fly to New York City and get married." She replied "Okay!"

Now, background here, we celebrate each other often. Not just on certain days or anniversaries. So it's not out of our norm to be so casual. Plus, when we were in different states and countries where gay marriage was legal, we'd talked about it. The subject was not too far out in left field. So we decided the time was perfect.

Before we married, I had the realization that I no longer wanted to keep my maiden name. I wanted to start fresh, start with my family, with my wife. I asked Cindy if I could take her name. She replied with tears that she would be honored. I asked her family if I could take on the family name. They loved it! I also made sure that my siblings were all right with it. Of course, they were happy for me, too.

It has never felt weird for me to take a different last name. From the start, we'd been "as one" anyway. I love being able to make a reservation under our name, rather than having to choose whose name it'd be under. I love being on a trip, and having our flight info be aligned. I love having our name on decorations around our home.

The little things. Things that are now every day, little things. Things that for hundreds of years, straight people took for granted.

There are so many things I love about being married. I still feel lucky every day to be with Cindy. She still continues to tick all my boxes, after all these years. And she still is funny as hell.

We are quirky and have our private jokes, and maybe our own private language. For example, we have fun with medical words. When there is no rush to get to sleep, we amuse ourselves saying the funniest anatomy word that we know. It's got to be correct, and it has to be within 30 seconds when it's your turn. Olecranon process. Sphenoid wing. We laugh and laugh.

I love her so much, it's beyond words. Cindy knows things that I've done in the past. And she does not care. As a matter of fact, she loves me because of what I've done, as it makes me who I am today. I've done some shitty things when I was young. I was sowing my oats, and not going about it the best way. Cindy is able to joke about it, saying "All of Austin has seen your boobs!" We'll meet someone, and I'll tell her later that it was either an ex of mine, or someone I'd gone on a date with. Her response is like no big deal. She's not threatened, because it's just information to her.

In 2014, my ex, Jenny, sent me a message, to tell me that she had cancer, a fast moving cancer. I still had so many unanswered questions about that relationship, knowing how strongly it affected me. Did she feel like I did, the split moment that we'd met? Had Jenny really loved me as much as I did her? I wondered if that relationship was as pivotal in her life as it was mine. Cindy told me to call Jenny, figure it out, talk it out, ask those questions, because otherwise I'd always wonder. That's the kind of wonderful that Cindy is.

Jenny began experimental treatments that extended her life well beyond the norm for her cancer, so over the next year, she and I went back and forth over it all. Sometimes painful, but for the most part caring and lovely. I don't ever wish to go back to those times with her, but I wish I'd acted differently. Smarter, kinder, more open minded to what she was going through during our relationship. When she died in 2015, she took a part of me with her. I was devastated. But that is okay. That is life. Over the next couple of months following her death, I felt a calmness that I'd not felt in the last seventeen years concerning her.

I realized before the one-year anniversary of her death that I'd almost forgotten it. I know now that what was taken from me with her death was the hold she'd had on me. The part of me that let someone have control over me, that codependence, was released. I now feel utter peace when I think of that relationship and when I think of her. It's wonderful.

I cannot thank Cindy enough for being so kind, so understanding, for being so open to what makes her life partner, me, tick. For making sure that my past tetherings are no longer there, making sure I feel completely satisfied in getting my answers.

Cindy is secure in herself, and in our relationship. She knows me, really knows me. She knows she can trust me. She knows my love and devotion for her. Years ago, I was planning to go to Dallas to see my beloved Concrete Blonde, with my friend Jason. Jason and I had been in Desert Storm together, and great friends before that and after that. I told Cindy that Jason and I had traveled all over together, and always snuggled when needed, even washed each other's backs. I wanted to make sure that if old times were continued, that it was okay. Cindy did not care. I love that. It shows why we work. There is not any jealousy. Cindy cares for Jason too and loves the history that I've shared with him. So while in Dallas, we were like two kids at a sleepover. It was a good night, jamming out at the concert, getting airborne in my little Mini on the way, and of course, snuggling and talking well into the night.

I have loved many people in my life, friends and otherwise, and still do. And nothing compares to the love of Cindy.

24

I talked earlier about sports, and so much of it is a mental game. When I started doing half-marathons in 2012, I did a number of them. I ran with the side of my left knee in pain for years. I finally figured out that my butt muscles needed to be strengthened. So it's important to have the muscles strong in all areas—and I realized that I ran on mental strength.

Having a good mindset is important, because if you tell yourself you can't, then you can't. I learned from Mom, too, about that. When she got lung cancer in 2015, her attitude kept her sane, and kept her pushing forward. She's still kicking to this day. I appreciate patients like that. If our positive energies are aligned, we can do so much more together.

When my nephew Cole died in 2017, I stopped running for a couple of months. When I started running again, I decided to do it for Cole, and for Vic. Cole could not run, ever. And Vic could not hardly walk, let alone run. How selfish of me to not run, when I was able bodied. After dealing with Cole's death, my mind was stronger, my faith in God and in myself was stronger. I decided to do a full marathon for my 50th birthday, which was in 2018. Cindy said she was in too, and she joined a local running group. My work hours do not allow me to get my money's worth out of joining up locally with runners so I joined an online running group. I also went to a running laboratory. They did a video of me running, and over the next month or so, helped me run better with their analysis of my issues. I did physical therapy, and a lot of painful massage. Being a preemie, wearing those leg braces, that was the reason I had issues with my legs and muscles. At age 49, I was finally learning how to retrain my legs to function better.

Running so much, for such long distances took a lot of mental strength. I had to remind myself the "why" over and over again. I remember one shitty Saturday, running a 16-miler or something, not wanting to finish it. A friend's husband had died the day before. So as I ran along, my mantra was, this is for Frank, this is for Cole, this is for Victor. It got me through it. I joined virtual half-marathons for various charities. I sent a photo of my first finishing medal, and the bib that I'd worn, with the name "Cole" on it, to my brother and his wife. I ran eight half-marathons from February to September 2018, all with the name "Cole" on my bib.

Cindy and I ran the Marine Corps Marathon that October. I'd just turned 50, and she was approaching her 50th two weeks after that. It was marvelous to start the race out together, to be around those amazing Marines, soldiers, family of military, all of it. My wife is a Marine, my uncle is a Marine, Cindy's niece and nephew are Marines. It was extraordinary. I ran for Cole, I ran for Victor.

I've learned a lot about physical and mental strength. I still need to grow in both areas. I'm happy that I am still learning. Pushing through when I may not be proud of what I've done, but I know that I am moving forward. Truly, that is all we can ever expect of ourselves.

Maybe the most important thing I have learned is that LIFE is a mental game.

Writing helps me with my mental game. That is why journaling has been such an important tool for me. And writing this book has been good for me. I write for me, yes, and I write for you. I believe this book is for many people. For sure, this is for people who don't think they are deserving. For some reason, I see a pattern with people. A pattern that they are not deserving. Myself included.

Who has taught us that we are not deserving of happiness, of reaching our goals?

You deserve to have a great life! First up, you have to take care of you. You have to put yourself first. It's not selfish, it's survival. Do what you need to do for you. No matter if you have 5 minutes to step outside and take a deep breath, or you take 30-60 minutes for a mind-clearing run or walk, you have to do something for you. Know that you are worth it. We are all worth it. Tell yourself every day. Show yourself every day.

Sometimes people that are the most giving to others, the most available to others, are not as kind to themselves. You know who you are. We all have responsibilities that sometimes make us think we have to take care of everyone and everything, before we ever do anything for ourselves. I see the self-care struggle. That is why I am here to kick you to do it.

Sometimes, when we do not take care of ourselves, our needs, our desires, we can end up feeling lost. We feel trapped or helpless or hopeless.

I am here to tell you there is always hope.

And I have to make mention: If you have thoughts of suicide, don't do it. You will get past it. I've seen it. I've done it.

I don't mean that you will "get over it." I mean, it's outside of you. Outside influences. So you have to go within.

Suicide prevention is just that. It's prevention. It's not some coined phrase or hashtag. It's actual prevention.

When you are in despair, remember that it's situational. Situations change. I'm not saying that I am stronger than others who contemplate suicide. I just happened to figure out that I should change my situation. I figured out what worked for me. What I still use as my way out of bullshit depression. Sadness. Fear.

There is a way out, and we all need to figure out what works for each of us.

It makes me angry. We are not born into despair and wanting to kill ourselves. There are layers upon layers of shit that happens for a person to get to this point.

Even if you have support, it often does not feel like it. Don't get me wrong, I had friends who said, "Reach out if you need something." It's hard to reach out when you feel like shit. I also had friends who said, "You are losing a lot of weight. Let's go to dinner." They didn't realize that I couldn't EAT dinner.

It's like the hospital when I was a child, trying to fix my legs. They put braces on my lower legs, but did not have the foresight to see that my issues stemmed from my hips. The issue starts somewhere else. It comes out in different ways. So find where your issue starts. And take care of you. Focus on you.

All I can say is hang on. Things can get better.

25

Well, that's it. For now. It has felt good to share pieces of my life with you, and I hope it has somehow made you feel more normal, and more understood. Is this "great wisdom?" Maybe not. But you can use it!

I've been asked for a couple of decades by various friends and acquaintances to write a book. It has been fun for me to jot this shit down. I called this project my "Bullet Points of Bullshit" and maybe I'll start a YouTube with that name.

Thanks for reading.

Let me close with an entry from my journal, from 1998:

There's ways to get through and I know there will be much pain in this life, but that's no reason to avoid all of the wonderful things.

We must do what we need to find these.

About the Author

Desiree is a native Minnesotan, but like many, she settled in a warmer climate to keep her toes thawed year-round instead.

She has three national certifications in medical imaging, useful in her mainly Pediatric MRI work. Her spare time is filled with being a Mini Cooper Car Club Organizer, Animal Communicator, and an athlete who enjoys mentoring.

Desiree lives with her wife, their circus of three cats and three Mini Coopers in Texas. Connect with Desiree at desireeakerlof@gmail.com or find her on YouTube at Des and Dat.

Editor's Note

I have never before inserted a note in a client book. But Desiree is unique. She told me she could drive a car while talking on the phone, smoking a cigarette, eating a popsicle, and painting her toenails. I don't think she was kidding.

She reached out stating she might want to write a book. In one short conversation, Desiree decided to go for it and was all in. She sent 3,000 words that night. Within two weeks, Desi had written 50,000 words—while working full-time, spending time with her wife and extended family, traveling, gardening, running, working out, managing the car club and several other projects. Desiree writes fast, talks fast, thinks fast. She likes to do many things at once, including self-reflection and extrapolating and explaining.

Her stories are hers, and universal. When sharing moments of life, Desiree's "it was nothing, but it was everything" point of view hits home.

Desiree literally wears her heart on both sleeves (her left arm is direct ancestors' signatures and her right arm is love notes from her wife and her siblings) and she shares her heart beautifully in these pages. She knows she is here to help people, and I know she can do that in a plethora of ways.

We decided to keep the editing of this book to a minimum and just let her talk. If you are having coffee with someone, one story leads to another. That is Desi's way. I invite you to spend time with Desiree, in her writing, on her podcast or YouTube or whatever she decides to do. She can do it all. And now she has just written her first book.

www.ingramcontent.com/pod-product-compliance
Lightning Source LLC
Chambersburg PA
CBHW030908080526
44589CB00010B/197